THINGS SEEN AND Unseen

Lawrence S. Cunningham is that rare person: a renowned scholar who not only writes beautifully, but whose essays, reviews, and books are useful. Reading Cunningham is like listening to an exceedingly wise, articulate, provocative, funny, and, above all, compassionate man who passionately wants you to meet the God he knows so well. Everything he writes is worth reading—often over and over. Highly recommended!

James Martin, S.J.

Author of *The Jesuit Guide to (Almost) Everything*

Airplane travel is notoriously awful, but every so often the fates smile and you end up next to a sparkling conversationalist—erudite yet unpretentious, utterly hilarious, the kind of person who even hiccups in epigrams. On those rare occasions, you hope the landing never comes. Lawrence Cunningham is just such a personality, and reading *Things Seen and Unseen* is like taking the trip of a lifetime in his company. Settle in and enjoy the ride!

John L. Allen Jr.

Senior Correspondent, *National Catholic Reporter*

For decades, Lawrence S. Cunningham has enlightened students and readers with the fruits of his academic discipline and his generous, reflective spirit. These excerpts from his notebooks convey not only his rich understanding of the Christian vision, but also his grasp of history, theology, and tradition vis-a-vis contemporary thinkers and events. Cunningham combines an intuitive sense of the holy and of beauty with care for the poor and a practiced life of prayer. His "jottings" will challenge, but also set the reader at ease. They demonstrate how delightful it can be to serve the Lord and others with full mind and heart and soul.

Patrick Jordan

Managing Editor, *Commonweal*

If you like Lawrence Cunningham's monthly reviews in *Commonweal*, you will love this book. Here we meet a theologian in his daily vocational practice as a scholar in love with Christian intellectual and artistic life, a Catholic who worships, prays, meditates, a teacher with a pastoral touch, an academic called on for lectures and talks and comments for the media, a voracious reader, a curious traveler, a kind and gentle man. Asked his goal as a teacher Cunningham first says "to convey a love of learning," then shyly refers to a well-known text, "the love of learning and desire for God." In these journal notes we meet a remarkable teacher who gracefully bears witness to that love and desire.

David J. O'Brien

Professor Emeritus, Holy Cross College

Things SEEN AND Unseen

A Catholic Theologian's Notebook

Lawrence S. Cunningham

SORIN BOOKS  Notre Dame, Indiana

Four lines of "Veni Creator" ("Come, Holy Spirit") from *The Collected Poems: 1931-1987* by Czeslaw Milosz. Copyright © 1988 by Czeslaw Milosz Royalties, Inc. Reprinted by permission of HarperCollins publishers.

www.sorinbooks.com

ISBN-10 1-933495-25-1   ISBN-13 978-1-933495-25-5

Cover image © Davy Kestens/stock.xchng.

Cover and text design by Andy Wagoner.

Printed and bound in the United States of America.

Library of Congress Cataloging-in-Publication Data

Cunningham, Lawrence.

Things seen and unseen : a Catholic theologian's notebook / Lawrence S. Cunningham.

    p. cm.

 ISBN-13: 978-1-933495-25-5 (hardcover)

 ISBN-10: 1-933495-25-1 (hardcover)

 1. Spirituality--Catholic Church. 2. Spirituality--United States. 3. Theologians--United States. 4. Catholic Church--Doctrines. I. Title.

 BX1406.3.C85 2010

 230'.2092--dc22

                                        2010015308

Introduction

For almost all of my two decades teaching theology at the University of Notre Dame, I have kept a reading and reflection notebook. I keep it in order to jot down interesting quotations, to think out fleeting ideas or thoughts that have occurred to me, to mark things I have seen or my reactions to them, to muse over books and articles I have read, to note random thoughts that occur while walking across campus, etc. Keeping this log has been one of the few disciplines I have maintained with some regularity over the years. Reading journals and diaries of other people has always been a pleasure to me, so it struck me that others might like a peek into the vagrant workings of one theologian's mind.

What appears in this book is an idiosyncratic sample, gleaned here and there, from a row of notebooks that sit on a shelf over my computer. This sample does not include the many verses (or two) of scripture I have written down over the years. Those verses have been—and here I borrow a conceit made famous by Matthew Arnold—"touchstones," which is to say, words so powerful that they stand for something much larger than is first seen in the words themselves. Certain lines of scripture have this in common with really great poems: paraphrasing them, or taking a stab at their exegesis (or even their eisegesis) is never really adequate as a replacement for the words themselves. I often write these biblical verses down

simply because they strike me, but as I cannot adequately re-
produce the inspiration that gave rise to my writing them in
the first place, I have not added them here.

It is obvious to me now that frequently these brief entries
were first steps toward essays I hoped to write but never got
around to finishing, although in a few instances some of the
lines do appear in one or other published place in a far different and expanded format and, usually, as part of a larger
argument. Other entries became incorporated into lectures,
either in the classroom or in other venues. A few became expanded within chapters of one or another of my books. On
more than one page, they were simply jottings of nice lines
I had read—passages from books or essays that struck me or
peculiar words that were curious or new. Many of these frag-
ments come from the books I read while preparing to write
my "Booknotes" column for *Commonweal* magazine—a pleasant
chore I have done for over two decades.

No attempt has been made to date these entries. Where a
date is pertinent the reader will intuit the time or place from
the text itself. In the early 1990s I spent nearly two years tran-
scribing and annotating the personal journals of Thomas
Merton—journals composed by the monk between 1952 and
1960. I had already been keeping journals myself by then, but I
did so somewhat randomly, often writing things down in notebooks initially meant for other purposes. It was while working
on Merton that I decided to acquire a proper journal—this was

in 1993—to keep my jottings in one place. I was a bit more extravagant than Merton (he used plain legal pads), but I did not feel the constraint imposed on him by his vow of poverty. Unfortunately, unlike Ralph Waldo Emerson, that indefatigable keeper of journals, I never made indices to my entries, with the consequence that I can never quite seem to find the things that I am looking for.

It has been a real adventure to go back over these many pages in my spare time. It is from the perusal of these notebooks that these samples have been taken. I have kept the notebook in obedience to an admonition of Thomas Merton's advice "to contemplate with a pencil." In my case it was a pen because writing in a notebook seems too intimate a thing to do on the computer.

At the same time, I have resisted calling these jottings a "journal" or a "diary." Alberto Melloni, commenting on the journals of Yves Congar, sets out the model of a good diary: precise dates, completeness in telling a story, identifying one's sources, relevance of impressions. That description stabs at my heart. It is true that in my notebooks there are dates (sometimes abbreviated to the saint of the day) and that some source is usually mentioned. But by and large, these are notebooks and not journals; the French distinction helps; what I write is a *cahier* and not a *journal* because I have never been disciplined enough to write in my notebook every day.

Karl Rahner once was asked about his life as a Jesuit theologian; what he said, *mutatis mutandis* and to a far lesser degree, resonates with my own experience and my own life as I look back on it after nearly four decades of teaching at the university level: "I did not lead a life. I worked, wrote, taught, tried to do my duty and earn a living. I tried this ordinary way of serving God." Contained in this volume are slices from my ordinary way.

It is customary when writing an introduction to a book to thank a plethora of persons for reading the manuscript, catching infelicities of style or errors of fact and so on, but the plain truth is that I have shared these notebooks with nobody. As a result, I have to assume full responsibility for what is contained below. However, I am not free from the duty and the pleasure of expressing gratitude. After all, the University of Notre Dame supplied me with a livelihood, superb colleagues, a steady parade of wonderful young people to teach, a church within which to worship, a place for my own daughters to receive an education, and an academic environment that made it pleasurable to work. I am particularly grateful to John Cavadini, my chairman for well over a decade, and Cyril O'Regan, with whom I converse most days and from whom I learn so much. In addition, my position here has afforded me many opportunities to travel here and abroad to lecture, teach, attend conferences, and so on. There is no other academic institution where I would prefer to be. In addition, my family made coming home each day a joy and exhibited a more than small measure of tolerance for my distracted style of living, my incapacity to learn about practical matters, and my inordinate passion for books. Many monastic communities bade me welcome to stay with them on occasion, supplying their proverbial hospitality and love of silence as the locus of thinking. My thanks go also to Tom Grady of Sorin Books for taking a chance on this book and to Patrick McGowan who edited the manuscript with care and good humor.

To all who have been my life companions, especially my wife Cecilia, who shares with me our empty nest, and my dear daughters Sarah and Julia, now ensconced in the Big Apple seeking their fortune, I dedicate these pages.

From the
NOTEBOOKS

In the season leading up to Christmas, it would be nice to be in a monastery where we could sing the great O Antiphons at Vespers during the octave leading up to the feast. The seven titles of *Wisdom, Lord, Root of Jesse, Key of David, Rising Sun, King of the Nations*, and *Emmanuel* are redolent of Advent's resident prophet, Isaiah. They also provide a thickness to the theological meaning of Christmas itself. I particularly like the metaphor of the "Rising Sun" because it gives theological meaning to the fact that Christmas is celebrated after the longest day of the year—Christ the true sun (as an indirect "baptizing" of the pagan feast of the newborn sun?) who radiates his presence over the world.

It is very hard, given the helter-skelter nature of the "holiday," to focus on the great mystery of Christmas, but a deep recollection of the O Antiphons certainly could help. Perhaps some imaginative parish or perhaps the local cathedral could begin the custom of having festal vespers with the O Antiphons as a far more satisfactory way to bring back Christmas as a Christian feast—that might be a more imaginative structure than the banal "put Christ back into Christmas" campaigns that generally do nothing.

A later Christmas thought: The Advent and Christmas seasons would be a good time to read those wonderful odes written by Ephrem the Syrian so readily available in the volume on Ephrem in the *Classics of Western Spirituality*; they are especially good for all of their scriptural allusions. Most of the Syriac fathers were relatively untouched by philosophical language, which means, in essence, that their prayers, hymns, meditations, and so on are lushly biblical.

Of course, one of the "must dos" of Advent is to read Isaiah, which I do faithfully each Advent from the Liturgy of the Hours—I even do it when other readings are demanded for the Immaculate Conception feast. I hope it is not ungenerous to think (as I do) that the feast of the Immaculate Conception is an intrusion into Advent.

An Epiphany Reflection

Christian art has had a long love affair with the Magi who bring gifts to the child Jesus. There is a tradition of depicting three visitors to Bethlehem that is as old as the catacomb frescos of the late third century. We presume three visitors because there were three gifts. Even though some later accounts multiplied the number of Magi, artists have stayed with three; after all, Matthew's gospel tells us of three gifts, even if it does not indicate how many Magi there in fact were.

In the Ravenna church of Sant'Apollinare Nuovo in the mosaics of the fifth century, the Magi march forward toward a regal Madonna with the child Jesus on her lap; they are all decked out in oriental dress and Phrygian caps. Their traditional burial place is said to be the crypt of the cathedral in

Cologne. Of course, in the Renaissance it was not unusual for a patron to pay for a scene of the Magi, since that afforded the patron to place his own portrait as one of them, as famously occurred in the de' Medici-financed "Visit of the Magi," by Sandro Botticelli.

The Magi are mysterious personages who "come from the East," but the Gospels tell us not too much about them. Decades ago Erich Auerbach famously argued in his book *Mimesis* that the Bible is all "foreground," thus leaving to the reader's imagination space to fill in the blanks as readers famously do when depicting, for example, what Jesus looked like. Hence, it is common to "make up" portraits of the Magi and "make up" their style of clothing.

I had the Magi in mind recently after reading something interesting in Saint Thomas Aquinas's commentary on the Gospel of Matthew during the Christmas break. While it has been traditional for commentators to link the gifts of gold, frankincense, and myrrh to the prophetic fulfillment of the life of Jesus as monarch, priest, and resurrected One, Thomas provides what, for him, is a staggeringly homely explanation of the gifts. He writes that the Magi brought gold because the Holy Family was poor; frankincense to take away the stench of the stable; and myrrh so that Mary could strengthen the limbs of the infant by anointing them. That would be an explanation one would expect from Saint Francis of Assisi, but from the cerebral Thomas? I think that such homely exegesis points out a deep truth that Aquinas instinctively understood: the Word really did become flesh; Jesus was a real human being; and the place where he was born probably did reek.

Aquinas's deep piety towards the humanity of Jesus (a hallmark of his century) is profoundly revealed in that small exegetical point. In the writings of Thomas it is wonderful to see revealed those little epiphanies of piety like his (did he smile when he did this?) division of his questions on the humanity of Jesus in the *tertia pars* of the *Summa* into thirty-three to honor the traditional number of years Jesus lived on earth. Obviously the great friar was not immune to the influence of popular piety.

Keeping with Auerbach's thesis (in his classic work *Mimesis*) of the penchant of the Bible to focus on foreground with little in the way of background is a useful notion to keep in mind. Recently I heard a homily at morning Mass here on campus. The gospel reading for the day was the story of the Prodigal Son. The celebrant argued that the parable of Jesus was particularly beautiful because it had such a happy ending: the prodigal was happy to be home; the elder son was reassured that he will receive his just inheritance; and the father was happy because his home was back in full harmony. I have heard that story since childhood and, truth be told, half-nodded through the homily (it was also very early in the morning), but listening to the reading and its exposition, it struck me that we cannot be satisfied with the conclusion of the homily since there were other characters in the story who might not have been happy, namely, the servants (literally according to the Greek: the slaves) who had to prepare the feast and, with the arrival of the returning son, had one more person after whom they had to clean and feed.

When Jesus first told that story, probably nobody adverted to the servants; they were just part of the furniture of life. What would have dumbfounded them was not that the son wasted his fortune (young men have done that throughout history); they would have marveled at a father who was the true prodigal! What father would have given a large chunk of the patrimony to an impertinently demanding youth? Of course, Jesus wanted the hearers to stop short when he told his story because he wanted to talk about the prodigal love of God who wantonly bestowed gifts on unworthy humanity. We have so domesticated the story that we miss that point and, in addition, overlook the slaves as well.

Saint Augustine read the story of the Prodigal Son at a profound level. Careful readers of the *Confessions* should note that the parable is a repeated theme in Augustine's book because he sees himself as the one who had gone out to a far country only to return to God after a life of wallowing in the pigsties of Carthage, Rome, and Milan. The "far country" becomes a metaphor for everyone who is far from God.

Pope Benedict XVI thinks that the parable is better titled "The Two Brothers," while recently I heard a wonderful homily arguing that it is the parable "of the Father." These readings only go to point out that classics like that parable possess a "surplus of meaning."

A wonderful quatrain from Czeslaw Milosz:

Come, Holy Spirit,
Bending or not bending the grasses . . .
I am only a man; I need visible signs.
I tire easily building the stairway of
abstraction.

The early pagan writers who commented on Christianity did not call the Jesus movement a religion but a *superstitio*— a superstition. This was the usual term found in Tacitus, Pliny, and Suetonius. Cicero had earlier bragged that while the Romans were known for their piety among the nations, they had a loathing for superstitions, which they would have understood as a form of religion run wild and, more dangerously, an erosion of that spirit of *pietas* to which the Roman state made to the gods.

Reading recently Newman's *An Essay on the Development of Christian Doctrine,* I discovered that he has many fine pages on this Roman discrimination between religion and superstition with copious citations from the Latin authors. It was only at the end of that rather long excursus that I discovered that Newman was just not recording history but making a polemical point. All the charges the Romans made against the superstitions of the Christians were the same accusations that the Protestants (and his fellow Anglicans or, as he would call them later in his Catholic days, "The National Church") made against Roman Catholicism in the nineteenth century: excessive devotional practices, the superstitions—there is no other adequate word for it—connected to popular religious rites, the enslavement of the mind, the excessive focus on expiation of sin, the craven following of a priestly caste, and so on. These are charges that the less genteel kinds of anti-Catholics make to this day. Newman wrote those pages, of course, early in 1845—the year he would be received into the Catholic Church; but he had waxed eloquently on the difference between religion and superstition in one of his university sermons years earlier.

Newman was not only a great apologist; he was a subtle and wicked polemicist.

——————————■——————————

An article that I read years ago by the late philosopher Susanne Langer on the aesthetics of music made the point (somewhat paradoxical until one thinks about it for a moment and then it becomes banal) that all music is heard against the background of silence. Music enters into silence (think of the opening chord of a Mozart symphony) and ends in silence (how irritated I get when the audience starts clapping before we hear those last notes ease off into silence), but the full performance is played against silence. It struck me then, and I have often meditated on it subsequently, that there is a good analogy here relative to God and creation: the world emerges from the silence of God and, finally, will return to God (the old theme of *exitus/redditus*) and thus we experience God as Silence against creation. In a paradoxical sense, then, we "hear" God in the interim as hearing silence in music. Why this strikes me as a good notion—though an imperfect one—is that it insists that God is both imminent in the world (the *Grund* as the medieval mystics like Eckhart would have it) but also transcendent in the sense that you have to hear music and silence simultaneously, just as you have to see creation and God at the same time, with God being as elusive as the silence in music. Without silence in the background indirectly experienced by musical pauses, music becomes cacophony; without God, creation becomes meaningless. Toying around with this idea has given me a deeper insight into lines like the verse in the

Psalms saying, "Be still and know that I am God." It has also helped me thicken my approach to writers like Saint John of the Cross who says, in his "Sayings of Light and Love," that God has uttered only one Word and one must hear that Word in silence.

Apropos of the need to reflect on silence is the late Iris Murdoch's observation that the curse of deafness is that one cannot hear the silence. That observation, like Langer's, is only paradoxical on first reading; when considered for a moment it becomes an empirical observation.

And this from Karl Jaspers: "The silence of fulfilled speech." That line could apply to the Logos. Some of the best writing on silence is to be found in Karl Rahner's early work *Encounters with Silence.*

Reading Octavio Paz on Sor Juana Inés de la Cruz I ran across a quatrain she wrote, pleading for the life of a condemned prisoner; it is apropos of our penchant for executing people so blithely in this country:

> Any man can take a life
> But only God can breathe in
> Thus only through the gift of life
> May you hope to resemble God.

Sor Juana was a *comfortable* nun equipped with a nice apartment, including a seemingly capacious study where she did her writing, a goodly collection of books, and a serving girl to take care of the mundane duties of daily living.

---■---

Cassian, in the *Institutes*, says that the goal (*skopos*) of the monastic life is "purity of heart"—I like his take on it much better than Evagrius's notion of *apatheia*, which comes too close to the English sound of "apathy." Of course, Cassian uses the term because the Beatitudes say that the one who is pure of heart shall see God. The opposite of purity of heart is what the Epistle of James calls being "double-souled" (*dipschoi*) in 1:8 and 4:8. The New American Bible (NAB) translates the phrase as "two minds"—a flaccid stab at the meaning. The Jerusalem Bible (French) reads the divided (*partagée*) soul—much nicer, as usual. Those divisions war within themselves, as Paul beautifully put it in Romans 7. I use the NAB in class out of loyalty to its American Catholic origin, but it is a flat, tone-deaf, read. It is so soulless a rendering of the Psalms that I have taken, given my modest linguistic skills, to reading the Psalms in Latin or in the French of the *Bible de Jerusalem* when piously inspired to do so; such inspiration comes, alas, all too infrequently. The late Richard John Neuhaus often lamented in print about the flatness of the NAB and, while I did not much agree with Neuhaus on many points, on that criticism I was with him.

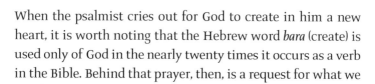

When the psalmist cries out for God to create in him a new heart, it is worth noting that the Hebrew word *bara* (create) is used only of God in the nearly twenty times it occurs as a verb in the Bible. Behind that prayer, then, is a request for what we would call "grace." Ezekiel has God promising that he is going to provide a spiritual transplant by excising a stony heart and providing a caring one.

The *Catechism of the Catholic Church*, in its fourth section on prayer (the best part of the catechism in my judgment), notes that the word "heart" occurs over a thousand times in the Bible. While preparing some retreat notes for a Benedictine community in New Jersey, I went through the Psalter and marked every place where the word "heart" occurs—it is a staggering number and widely used in context.

We have a spillover in our own usage: "cold-hearted" or "hard-hearted" or "heartless" and so on. Saint Francis de Sales would ask people: "How is your heart?"

Some years ago, when the Trappists at Gethsemani were celebrating their 150th anniversary, there was a display in the cloister of documents, old photographs, and artifacts, including a stained glass window depicting the Blessed Mother squeezing her breast from which a long stream of milk shot in an arc into the waiting mouth of Saint Bernard of Clairvaux, who was depicted in the next panel. It was a piously hilarious scene now kept safely out of common view somewhere in the recesses of the monastery. It was a somewhat overwrought adaptation of the *Virgo Lactans*, which often enough appears in late medieval art. At the shrine in St. Augustine, Florida, one can venerate the *Virgen de la Leche y Buen Parto*—a statue showing Mary nursing the Christ child—known in English as the Virgin of Milk and Safe Delivery. There is a figure of Mary in the Church of San Agostino in Rome where, it is said, Roman women go to pray when they want to conceive a child. Further: I was once shown a vial in a collection of relics containing some of the Virgin's milk (was it at the Church of Santa Maria in Via Lata in Rome?). Those kinds of sentiments have deep and, possibly, pre-Christian roots in Catholic piety (I rather enjoy running across them) but the stained glass windows at Gethsemani were just a bit over the top.

A reporter for some newspaper interviewed me by phone about the role of angels in Christianity. She was writing a story about the popular interest in angels (an interest now fading as most fads do). This was the time when people were running seminars on how to get in touch with your angel; when shops were full of angel junk; when really atrocious books on angels made the best-seller lists—in other words, it was a raging fad now thankfully passed. After asserting that Christianity was not centrally about angels (as the Epistle to the Hebrews makes abundantly clear) I went on to give her the standard material about the role of angels in Catholic life and doctrine. As we were winding down our conversation, she asked me if I personally believed in angels. I typically hate these requests for personal professions of faith but the opportunity was too delicious to pass up. My answer, basically, was that after death I am going to be mightily disappointed if there were no angels. I had begun praying to my guardian angel ("Angel of God, my guardian dear . . . , etc.") at—when? The age of five? That euphonious prayer had been in my head ever since.

Later addendum: A German theology professor from Potsdam was a recent visitor here at Notre Dame. He is writing a book on angels, inspired, he told me, because a recent poll in Germany indicates that more Germans believe in angels than in God. Could that be?

Early devotional practices, once learned, never quite leave us. A nun once told me in an elementary school catechism class to say "Jesus mercy" every time I heard a siren, since the ambulance or fire truck or squad car was responding to a need.

I have kept that practice up for years, and it is not a trivial matter since our home is a stone's throw away from the city's largest emergency ward.

Are these pious superstitions? I think not. They are all practices that keep alive the "memory of the Lord"—a way of living in God highly recommended by the early fathers of the church. There is a way in which the memory of the Lord is the notion behind the ordinary exercises of piety: morning and evening prayers and a blessing before meals are wonderful examples of ways in which the quotidian becomes punctuated by the memory of the Lord—they are ways of becoming re-collected. It is here where the Buddhist practice of "mindfulness" (as taught, for example, by the Vietnamese monk Thich Nhat Hanh) is useful.

Apropos of the memory of the Lord: The Italian verb to remember is *ricordare*—literally it means: to bring back to the heart. How wonderfully rich etymology can be!

At an Ash Wednesday homily, the celebrant pointed out that we sign a cross on an infant's brow at baptism, and the priest makes the Sign of the Cross over a coffin at the end of life. In the interstices we make thousands of such signs. The Sign of the Cross (Tertullian mentions the custom) is an act of faith both in our redemption (the cross) and in the Trinity (the formula). I always remember a line from Romano Guardini (I have this feeling that I have written this down somewhere before) who says that we should always make a bold Sign of the Cross as a witness to our faith; the gesture should be clear and not some miserly waving the hand around. The Sign of the Cross is the Creed in shorthand.

The sixth century Irish saint Ida (a name almost never given to girls today) is said to have taught that the three things God loves most are faith in God with a pure heart; a simple life with a grateful spirit; and generosity inspired by charity. The three things God most despises are a mouth that spews hatred for people; a heart harboring resentment; and confidence in wealth.

A curious call today from a reporter from the *Wall Street Journal* in, of all places, Rio de Janeiro, asking me if I knew anything about Saint Expeditus. There is evidently a wild following of this saint in Rio with supplicants imploring either wealth or health but mainly wealth. As far as I can determine some relics were once shipped out of Italy to France with a marking on the box asking that they be "expedited"—somehow the name got attached to the relics and somehow the cult spread from France to Brazil. This is one of the more outlandish examples of name confusion in hagiography, like the case of the saint "Philomena" in the nineteenth century, but an interesting one nonetheless.

In his notebooks, Thomas Merton muses over a Saint Audactus who, according to the legend, starts following another martyr to the place of execution, confesses his own faith, and is also put to death. He was thus named *audactus*—"added."

A Few Jerusalem Impressions

Jerusalem the Golden. It is said that vast quantities of its characteristic stone are exported to places like New Jersey to build homes for wealthy Jewish families or to provide facing for synagogues.

The security wall: a vast tapeworm devouring acreage, groves, farms. It is staggeringly ugly and, beyond that, an affront to human dignity.

An ancient Arab tends a flock while helicopters buzz overhead. I watched him from the roof of the study center at Tantur, looking towards Bethlehem.

Ugly, tasteless neon lights festooning the tower of a mosque near Bethlehem. It flashes on and off as the call to prayer is blasted out over loudspeakers. The neon is really tacky.

A crow caws over the Church of the Holy Sepulchre. Little Sisters of Jesus in their shop on the Via Dolorosa. A radio station broadcasts the recitation of the Koran twenty-four-hours-a-day. A cab driver explained to me that the reciter was doing so in the "Meccan" style as we careened through the outskirts of Jerusalem.

Cats around the rose gardens of Tantur: feral, mean, and hostile. They slink around the rose bushes that have canes as thick as my arm. The roses are tended by an old sheikh with tender care and a green thumb.

The Catholic shrine churches under Franciscan care: uniformly decorated with mediocre mosaics or murals. They are generally tasteless—all done up, I have been told, by some Italian architects some decades ago.

After a few days: an eerie feeling that a life here could turn one into a religious zealot. It is said that, in fact, some do fall prey to the "Jerusalem Syndrome" and begin having messianic fantasies and so on. Evidently, they are carted off to some local psychiatrist who treats these delusions on a regular basis.

The poor Ethiopian monks who live in huts on the roof of the Church of the Holy Sepulchre. They are evidently despised by the Copts from Egypt. One of the Ethiopians moved his chair to get some shade a year or two ago and a fistfight broke out because a Copt saw the shift as an attempt to encroach.

A wonderful line from Isaiah: "O Jerusalem, I have set watchmen; all the day and all the night, they shall never be silent" (62:6). (A note to myself: make a set of quotes from the Bible in which Jerusalem is directly addressed, as when Jesus laments over the city: "Jerusalem, Jerusalem . . . , " etc.)

It was only after landing in Ben Gurion airport in Tel Aviv the second time that I adverted to the fact that when one leaves the airport for Jerusalem, one is driving upward. It was then that, for the first time, the "ascent" psalms took on vivid meaning for me, and the phrase "Mount Zion" took on a more vivid sense. Tel Aviv, by the way, is a dreary, modern city redeemed only because it is near the sea. It is a Hebrew-speaking Detroit.

In the nave of the Church of the Holy Sepulchre there is a marker (an alabaster vase) that marks the *ompholos*—the navel or center of the world.

Inside the Jaffa Gate eating lunch at an Arab-owned restaurant with very reluctant Jewish friends. Tensions are palpable.

The best souvenirs from Jerusalem are the Armenian tiles; alas, the one shop in the Armenian Quarter had shut down and the owner moved on, probably to Los Angeles. The one on the Via Dolorosa remains. The owner tells me that his grandfather was brought to Jerusalem to do repair work on the Dome of the Rock until it was learned that he was not a Muslim.

The Church of the Holy Sepulchre is not only ugly in its own right, but ugly in its atmosphere with the various sects quarreling for space. Over the purported tomb of Christ is the Latin tag, *Resurrexit. Non est hic.* Thomas Merton said, after reading of the quarrels in the sepulcher, "How true! How true!" In my many visits there I am disinclined to pray; I tend to wander around and gape. The church, despite its noble ancestry, is a very unedifying place. It is the one place in Israel (the recent security wall excepted) that truly depresses me.

To visit the buildings on the Temple Mount one pays a hefty fee—it probably helps with the salary of the attendant in the inside of the Dome of the Rock who patrols zealously to be sure that no non-Muslim is tempted to pray.

I usually enter the Old City through the Jaffa Gate when coming from Tantur, but my favorite entrance is the Damascus Gate—all crowded and bustling and redolent of the Middle East.

A favorite place to worship: with the Benedictines at the monastic church in the village of Abu Ghosh. A mixed community of men and women founded from Bec in France, there are a fair number of Africans in the community. The liturgy, with the common parts in Latin and the rest in French, is reverent and simple. Typically, on Sunday, while the community worships, the nearby mosque blasts out sayings from the Koran—as a countervoice to the worship of the "Franks."

It is a hallowed custom for a visitor to Jerusalem to bring a bit of money meant for the poor and donated by a Jew to give away while there. I typically unburden my dollars to a raggedy Hasid *schnorrer* who speaks decent English; he, in turn, gives me a candle to burn in the caverns just to the left of the Western Wall. I always light the candle. He is a Bratslaver Hasid and once invited me for a Sabbath meal, but I reluctantly had to decline the invitation. His long coat is spotted with candle wax and he has bad teeth, but his friendliness is genuine. I now possess a *kippah* so I do not have to use those cardboard ones they offer at the Wall—they almost always blow off at the slightest breeze.

I try to get to the Armenian church in their quarter for their Vespers even though I do not understand a word of Armenian. The last time I was there a companion was turned away because he had Bermuda shorts on. The Armenian museum is a bit tattered but surprisingly moving. Looking out the windows, one spots the vastly overgrown graveyard.

When the settlers come into town to visit the Western Wall, one sees that many of them carry UZI submachine guns slung over their shoulders by short bandoliers. Those that are so armed inevitably swagger about in a most disagreeable, snarling fashion; it is the guns that dictate the gait.

Every time I take the path (between the Armenian and Jewish quarters) to see the Benedictine monastery inside the Old City (overbuilt and looming), I run across some Nordic-looking guy dressed in robes strumming a stringed instrument of some sort a la David. Alas, he merely looks goofy.

I love strolling through Mea Shearim, the area of the *Haredi* (ultra-orthodox), listening for the droning and humming coming out of the (how many?) yeshivas in the area. A warning in Yiddish and English warns visitors to be decently dressed on the streets. Why do the *Haredim* never smile? Once I saw a poster showing a body gruesomely mutilated after an autopsy—the *Haredi* are against autopsies. Once when visiting Disney World with my family, the grounds were full of Hasidim from New York. The children were ecstatic; the women, with their wigs and floral dresses, festive; but the men seemed glum and wary. I suppose I would be glum also with a long black coat on in central Florida's stupefying heat.

It is odd that in my many visits to Israel I have never made it to the Galilee. Jerusalem and its environs hold me like a prisoner. I have this recurring fear that I will fall prey to the Jerusalem Syndrome of which psychiatrists speak and turn into some sort of religious fanatic. I get the same feeling in Rome sometimes and imagine myself living there in some little nook, spending my days wandering from church to church.

I just learned a great word, evidently coined by Leibniz: *psittacism*—the tendency to parrot back verbatim what one has received as, for example, the answers students give at a final examination.

Another good word: *tawdry*—it derives from Saint Audrey and first meant the trinkets sold at her shrine.

And: *saunter*—an old pilgrimage-inspired word—a *sainte terre* to the Holy Land.

Charles Williams in *The Descent of the Dove* said that the life of Saint John of the Cross "seems as if it were compensation for the glory of the Renaissance popes." That is so true, since John of the Cross had a single vision; as he said in one of his letters, "everything outside of God is narrow." What is most striking about John is that his own view was narrow but in a very good sense: he never wavered from his thirst for God. At a time in history when religious experience was sought with avidity, he asked people to reach beyond the experiential. He is alleged to have said that he would not walk across the street to see a stigmatic, and he was notoriously disinterested in things like visions, locutions, raptures, and the other epiphenomena of "mystical" experience. John's rigor in this area came from his conviction that people would seek out "experience" and, in the frisson of such experiences, seek them for themselves and, hence, would miss God. Part of John's resistance was also a reaction against the rise of people who so avidly sought after one kind of experience or another. Of course, his compatriot,

Saint Teresa of Avila, was far more indulgent about such experiences, as is clear from *The Interior Castle*; but even Teresa, after her description of the various mansions, ends up (near the end) saying that the criterion by which one judges the authenticity of experience is simply an affirmative answer to the question, "Do you love your neighbor more?"

John was active in the pastoral ministry; he taught catechism, took his novices on picnics, walked all over Spain in his ministry. Too many think of him holed up in a cell in ecstasy. He was a doer.

Edith Stein's book *The Science of the Cross* has excellent lines on John's use of the word "night." Contrary to almost universal citation, John himself never speaks of the "Dark Night of the Soul," but he does speak of the dark night of the senses and of faith. The word "night" is what Karl Rahner would classify as among the *Uwortes*—those primordial words that defy paraphrase: "Oh Watchman! What of the night?"

Here is a severe reproach to any serious theologian from an observation by Simone Weil: "To be able to study the supernatural one must first be capable of discerning it." Weil, of course, could be brutally realistic about such matters. Simone de Beauvoir, as she tells us in her autobiography, was a bit terrified of Weil in describing their youthful days as fellow students. I once read a perceptive essay by the late Susan

Taubes who, rightly, judged that Weil was a person to be admired from afar but never emulated. Saint Bonaventure said roughly the same thing about Saint Francis in his *Legenda Major* because Bonaventure knew that Francis was no sentimental hippie *avant la parole*. More recently, Caroline Bynum wrote that medieval hagiographers warned readers not to try and emulate the saints because their lives were too dangerous to imitate.

Every once in a while I teach Simone Weil, but most commonly Weil terrifies the students. I have an intense admiration for her, despite her rather unsmiling seriousness.

When I was among the guests at the monastic community of Bose in the mountains near Turin, Italy, there was a tower near our quarters with a beautiful crowing cock in bronze above the clock tower. On adjacent sides were these two beautiful Latin texts:

Jam gallus
Cantat fervidus
Et somnolentes
Increpat
Judicium Dei
Nuntiet.

(The cock sings insistently/jarring awake the sleepy/announcing the judgment of God.)

> *Vigilate quia*
> *Ne scitis quando*
> *Dominus veniet*
> *Sero*
> *An media nocte*
> *An galli cantu*
> *An mane*

(Watch/for you know not/when the Lord comes/in evening or midnight or cock crow in morning.)

The Latin lines are nicely rendered and fit well with the bronze rooster above the clock, but it came to my mind that the lines conceal a monastic trope—the monk as watcher. After all, it is not accidental that the night liturgical office is called "Vigils." Monastic life is profoundly eschatological—the monk testifies by form of life that there is a "not yet" to be reached—one is celibate for the good of the Kingdom; one shares all things in common as a sign of the future church in heaven; and so on. Reminder to myself: gather up those texts from the Bible describing the watchman (e.g., the image from the Psalms where the writer yearns for God in the way the watchman yearns for the breaking in of the sun on the horizon). See: Merton's meditation on the "Firewatch" at the end of *The Sign of Jonas.*

Later addendum: I found another allusion to the morning cockcrow in John Milton's *Carmina Elegiaca*: a plea for early rising because the rooster has already called *"invigilans ad sua quemque vocat"*—calling each to his task. These lines follow the urgent opening of the poem to "get up," "rise up," "throw off dreams," etc.

Kierkegaard says this about monasteries and monastic life: "The 'monastery' is an essential dialectical element in Christianity. We therefore need it out there like a navigation buoy at sea in order to see where we are, even though I myself would not enter it. But if there is really true Christianity in every generation, there must also be individuals who have this need."

Thomas Merton says somewhere that the night is the time of the monk. When I am a guest at Trappist houses, my favorite time of the day is the long interval that comes between the end of Vigils and the bell calling the monks back to church for Lauds. It is roughly the period from 4:00 a.m. to 6:00 a.m., in which the monk is free to do anything except go back to bed. At a monastery in the high desert below Tucson, it is the time to look up at the night sky for awhile. The desert sky is free of light pollution, and that means that not only do the stars and planets come into sharp relief, but the blackness of the night is rich beyond words—deep purple and velvety. One begins to

understand why mystics are drawn to the desert. I read somewhere that Saint Ignatius of Loyola, not a monk, to be sure,
frequently gazed up at the sky from his Roman roof (long before urban light pollution!). There is a good exhortation to be
composed on the theme of looking up at the sky. Children do
it in awe on summer evenings, and Hopkins wrote a sonnet
about it. We probably do not look up enough because we do
not get up early enough, and in the late night we are busy doing something or going somewhere or streetlights discourage
us or—worst of all—people might think we are frivolous.

The night interval allows one to think about other people
who are awake at that time who do not want to be awake: a
mother soothing a sick child; a husband drinking coffee in the
kitchen, wondering how he is going to make his car payment;
a street person wandering around; someone in too much pain
to sleep in a hospital bed. . . . To remember these people at that
hour is close to a prayer for and with them—an act of human
solidarity for those who are in need.

Even though Easter is *the* feast of Christianity, in popular
culture it is Christmas. The reason is not hard to discern.
Everyone can relate to the innocence of a child, but one can
only yearn for life after death. There is a profound mystery in
Christmas—the Word made flesh—but it is flesh that we understand. Easter, by contrast, touches the heart of mystery

by disconfirming the finality of death and oblivion. It is for that reason that Paul's great meditation on the Resurrection of Christ in 1 Corinthians 15 makes such a profound impression on me. It is Paul's adamantine insistence that if the Resurrection is not true, we are flapping our lips and wasting our time. Paul also understands that what we believe is hard to imagine—thus his reaching for the metaphor of, for example, the dying seed which brings forth new life.

As an aside: Paul's metaphor gives indirect warrant for the prominence of flowers at Easter.

Another aside: It is the Byzantine liturgy that best celebrates Easter: "By his death he has conquered death and given life to those who are in the tomb" is the repeated theme of the Easter liturgy. Byzantine Easter is theology as spectacle as well as proclamation.

And another: There is a subtle way in which the Christian East links the Nativity of Jesus and his Resurrection. Icons of the Nativity, typically, depict in the background an open cave. The symbolism is double: Jesus was born into mean circumstances (in the East, a cave instead of a stable since caves often doubled as stables), but the open cave also alludes to his death and Resurrection.

Later Addendum: I learn from reading some sermons on the liturgy by the great Russian Orthodox theologian Sergius Bulgakov that a Christmas hymn in the Orthodox liturgy refers to the "heaven-cave," to contrast the light of paradise giving way to the darkness of the cave where the infant is born.

Someday I want to think out on paper why Christmas somehow slightly depresses me. I hate the frantic buying and selling leading up to the day, and even though I love to belt out the old Christmas hymns at Mass, is there any time more sad than Christmas afternoon, the gifts having been opened, the hoopla over, and the only consolation being leftovers to make turkey sandwiches for the next day or so? It is all too much, and I think it has to do with all the buying and the unreasonable expectations. The best part of Christmas, apart from the beauty of the liturgy, is eating together as a family and with friends.

Truth demands I say, however, that I always like my Christmas gifts because both my wife and my daughters are savvy shoppers, whereas I am a lousy, impatient, and clueless one. Furthermore: I have very little imagination when it comes to gifts and, worse, I am a bit of a cheapskate and, finally, totally inept when it comes to wrapping up anything.

The other day a student complained to me about a language course he was taking: "All we do is grammar." Okay, I can

remember wrestling with the Greek middle voice while curs-
ing the tedium of "doing grammar," but grammar, widely
grasped, is the scaffolding of intelligibility—which is why
everyone from Newman to Wittgenstein uses the word in a
capacious sense. Without grammar we would have the bone
eating the dog.

Somewhere I ran across this line from Saint Peter Damien:
"Christ is my grammar" (*Grammatica mea Christus est*). What he
was saying is that Christ is the structure of his understanding of reality. Grammar, in that sense, provides the order that
makes intelligibility possible. Damien probably meant in context to quit fiddling with secular learning and learn Christ, but
he conveniently forgot that he had to learn grammar enough
to write Latin as well as he did.

Saint Bonaventure has an interesting symbol for Christ
that is an expansion of the notion of grammar: Christ as the
Book. Toward the end of the *Lignum Vitae*, he describes Christ
as a Book (the Book of Wisdom) and, he says, that Book consists of one Word. Toward the conclusion of that section, he
utters a kind of canticle of praise of what is contained in that
Book. I am on the lookout for other authors who use the same
symbol, but so far have not tracked any down.

Borges once mused that it would be interesting to think of
The Imitation of Christ as rewritten by James Joyce.

———————■———————

Patricia Hampl once opined in an essay contributed to a volume on martyrs that the inscription of Edith Stein in the canon of the martyr saints may have been a mistake; that she should stand "in between," as a sign of the need for Christian contrition—standing "forever as a ghost." I am not sure that I agree but I do see the point. Every time I think of Edith Stein I also think of that strange spiritual enigma, Etty Hillesum, who saw Edith and her sister at the Dutch transfer point of Westerbork before being shipped off to Auschwitz. Etty describes seeing them in a letter from Westerbork. Edith Stein was a Jew, but she did not convert to Catholicism from Judaism; she converted from atheism—a quite different matter. Stein reported that she converted, under the impulse of grace, after reading Teresa of Avila's autobiography. Teresa herself remarks in the same book that reading Augustine's *Confessions* was a turning point in her life; Augustine marks his conversion happening after reading a codex of Paul's letters. Conversion *ex libris*! What a chain: Paul to Augustine to Teresa to Edith.

The complete version of Hillesum's diaries has recently been published. It was very painful to read them; the entries were dated and she often would remark about the tightening restrictions being placed on Amsterdam's Jews (no riding bicycles, no entering grocery stores, etc.). One reads while saying to oneself: "Don't you know what is ahead for you?" Her last piece of writing was a postcard thrown out of a boxcar on its way east. Some good soul mailed it for her. Hillesum's diary reflects a young woman possessed of a robust sexuality in tandem with a deeply mystical bent.

I could barely finish Ray Monk's first volume of his biography of Bertrand Russell. Russell was a snob—cold, priapic, and so on. While visiting Verona on an Italian tour, battered by Wittgenstein's critique of his philosophical positions, his separation from Ottoline Morrell (another piece of work!), and terrified that he was going crazy, he thought that maybe he should try to become a saint. He actually tried to pray in the Church of San Zeno. The mood evidently did not last. As brilliant as he was (until he turned into a writing hack), his notions about religion were unremittingly banal. He was an awful person; even pictures of him repel me. (Monk's biography of Wittgenstein was brilliant; one of the best biographies I have ever read.)

In one of his essays, Francis Bacon spoke of books only to be tasted. I read too many books too quickly and, for the most part, pass them on to students or otherwise give them away. Some books one reads over and over again. Robert Wilken spoke to my class on Augustine's *Confessions* and said, wisely, that the Augustine one reads as an undergraduate is not the same Augustine one reads as an adult. That is undeniably true. My battered Penguin copy of Augustine, translated by an English scholar with the risible surname of Pine-Coffin, is scribbled all over; the pages fall out, so reluctantly I began rereading a new translation by Maria Boulding. It is like discovering Augustine all over again. Sometimes I read Augustine in Latin—a wonderful practice because his Latin is demanding, which means that one reads slowly, not allowing the eye to skim down the page as one does at times when reading in English.

The books I tend to keep are reference books. Recently someone—generous soul!—gave me a full set of the *Oxford English Dictionary*, which is my favorite volume to browse. I gave away my two-volume set (readable only with a magnifying glass) and now can savor the heft of the regular version. I have always wanted to have a full set because somewhere I read that W. H. Auden kept a volume at his table and skimmed through it while having breakfast each morning. That certainly beats my practice of reading the local paper that, more times than not, has very little of interest.

One of the things I like about Newman's spirituality is his emphasis on doing the ordinary well: getting up, offering the day to God, etc. When, in his later years, in the full flush of Roman fever on the part of some Anglo-Catholics, someone asked Newman about taking the discipline, Newman replied that in his estimation, the greatest discipline was "to do well the duties of the day." I cannot even imagine Newman whipping himself, although as a young man he fasted so assiduously as to nearly imperil his health.

I have been reading Newman for over forty years, and one of the pleasant things about reading him is that often, in the midst of those long Ciceronian passages (how Newman loves the semi-colon!) one runs across a brief, pungent sentence that is clearly eligible to be called an aphorism. I have jotted down dozens of them over the years. Just recently, this, from the *Tamworth Reading Room*: "Religion has never been a deduction from what we know; it has ever been an assertion of what we are to believe." In a nutshell, that stipulates what Newman felt was wrong with what he called "liberalism" (see the appendix in the *Apologia*)—namely, the notion that reason judges the rightness of belief. Rather, like Anselm and others: *credo ut intelligam*.

For preparation for a doctoral seminar (and a little anthology of Newman texts) I read all the volumes of the *Parochial and Plain Sermons* over the course of a semester. There is a goldmine of MA and PhD theses in those sermons. Interestingly enough, I found only a couple of rare occasions when Newman quoted any book other than the scriptures. He himself said that his sermons (preached at Saint Mary's in his Anglican days) never spoke of the great controversies with which he was engaged at the time. Newman's *Parochial and Plain Sermons* would be at the top of my list for the "best" of spiritual reading.

Half jokingly, I tell students when we begin studying Newman that they may learn a little theology from him, but they will learn a lot about what a great English sentence looks like. Discussing all this with a graduate student who told me of a Newman search engine that, when a phrase is punched in, rarely turns up more than three or four instances. The conclusion: almost everything that he wrote was fresh; he did not repeat himself much.

After Newman died, one of his Oratorian confreres said that the community had few gossipy things to say about him and few anecdotes to reminisce about his crochets, idiosyncrasies, and so on. The point his confrere was urging was that Newman led an ordinary life—how extraordinary! He was not a "personality" or a "character"—that is a status to which one could aspire.

Some years ago on the day of an important football game (but not so important that I can remember the name of the team we were playing) here at the Notre Dame stadium, the television producers used the repeated conceit of depicting a flickering candle at the grotto to heighten the importance of the game for the Notre Dame faithful. I hate that kind of pious claptrap! This reduction of religious faith to these sorts of banalities does more harm to the Church than can be imagined. I was tempted to walk over to the grotto and light a candle (or, at least, to blow one out) with the hope that we would lose the damn game! (I resisted the temptation.)

This is not to say that I think the grotto on campus is in its own right banal. In fact, it is a real "sacred space" (Mircea Eliade), and it is a rare moment—day or night—that there is not at least one person sitting there or kneeling in prayer. Newly married couples pose for pictures, small groups say the rosary, seniors visit there before graduation; it is alleged to be *the* spot to get engaged. It is quiet and has an aura that is almost palpable. When a good friend of mine was stricken with brain cancer, I lit more than one candle and am not ashamed to say so. Often, on a late afternoon, I go over there and sit on one of the benches to read after walking around the lake. The grotto is at its most beautiful when the snow is deep on the campus—the banks of candles cast odd lights over the pristine white.

There is something quite atavistic about the impulse to create such spaces. Right after the horrible events of 9/11, the makeshift shrines were in evidence almost immediately: photos, flowers, candles, messages. Interesting question: why do people do that? Such a question is profoundly theological, no matter what else it might be.

In my work on the saints over the years, I have become in-
trigued by the titles that certain saints in the Byzantine
world are given. Thus, Saints Cosmas and Damien are called
the "moneyless ones" because they did not charge for their
medical services. Saint Marcellus is one of the *akoimetoi*, the
"non-resting ones," so named for their assiduous life of constant prayer. I love the title given to those who faced violence
without resisting, like the brothers Saints Boris and Gleb in
Russia—they are the "passion bearers." Perhaps the oddest are
the monks at Saint Saba in the ninth century, who were up-
holders of the veneration of icons. Iconoclastic monks incised
lines of scripture on their faces—according to Butler, twelve
lines of iambic verse!—so they became known as the *graphtoi*:
the "written ones." Two of them were brothers, Theodore and
Theophanes.

R. G. Collingwood once said this about an Oxford seminar:
one of the company reads a paper, and the rest discuss it with
a fluency directly proportional to their ignorance. This is a
phenomenon not unknown at my own university.

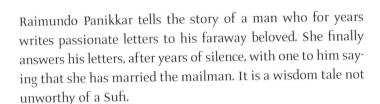

Raimundo Panikkar tells the story of a man who for years writes passionate letters to his faraway beloved. She finally answers his letters, after years of silence, with one to him saying that she has married the mailman. It is a wisdom tale not unworthy of a Sufi.

In discussing the annunciation to Mary in class with my freshmen students, it is clear that they understand that an angel appeared as a visual reality to her, that she saw an angel. That way of understanding things is fully understandable because of the powerful impact of art upon our way of reading scripture. Now, it may well be that Mary saw an angel (*aggelos* —messenger) or that Luke understood that to be the case or, maybe, he used the figure of an angel to mean that a divine message was being conveyed to Mary. When we speak of people having visions (we get mail from such people now and again) we, or better, they, tend to think that the visions are like projections outside the person and, again, the impact of art is powerful here. However, it is clear in reading someone like Julian of Norwich's *Showings* that she has a quite diverse vocabulary to describe her own experiences.

Julian speaks of an interior word or an intuition deep within herself (a kind of profound insight) or, in the case of

seeing the suffering Christ which opens her book, it is linked
to the cross bearer who comes with the priest to give her the
last rites—a sort of hyper visualization of something actually
there. These various communications she calls, in her English
dialect, "shewings." Julian's vocabulary is in some fashion in
debt to the discriminations Saint Augustine made when he
discussed the various theophanies in the Bible. He treats such
matters in his commentaries on Genesis. We had a very good
dissertation written on this Augustinian theme a few years
ago. Sometimes the use of the term "vision" is, in fact, a generic term that covers a lot of ground, as is clear from a careful
reading of Julian. When teaching that text I have sketched
out the taxonomy of ways in which she speaks of her "showings." They are very sophisticated.

In conjunction with this topic one recalls what is commonly called the "Vision at Ostia" narrated by Augustine in
the *Confessions*. As James O'Donnell pointed out in his exhaus-
tive commentary on the text, what Augustine and his mother
experienced was not so much a vision but an audition; it is
not what they saw but what they heard (paradoxically, silence!) that is the common thread of the text.

This is of great interest to me because of my interest in
the ways in which art, in all its forms, and the human imagination that feeds on art, so shape the way in which we discuss
religious topics. When people inquire of me about angels or
demons—to cite an obvious example—they come with the

prior conception of androgynous figures with wings or horned creatures with pitchforks, and it is only when we abstract our discussion from such images that the topic can be explored. This is all the more important when we go deeper into the reality of God.

If God is conceived of as the "Man upstairs"—never adverting that in our world after Newton and Einstein there is no "up"—then all sorts of problems emerge. I would not allow a child to have a fatal cancer—why can't the "Man upstairs" do something about that? I am no great cheerleader for Bultmann, but I appreciate his conviction that we read the New Testament wrongly if we too literally conceive of it in terms of the now discredited three-deck universe.

To borrow from the language of Paul Ricoeur, we have to shed that understanding which reflects first naiveté in order to get at religious truth at the level of second naiveté. In other words, people have had and will continue to have visions, but they will be pictures "out there." Or, to say it differently, Mary received a message from God not quite the way Fra Angelico depicts it, but both he and the gospel writer got it right in their own way. My conviction that this is true is derived from the old patristic sense that the Bible has a "mystical" meaning, that is, something that lies hidden under the plain sense of the text. The fathers used the word "mystical" to describe, among other things, the Eucharist (what is real is hidden under what is apparent), and the Church. They also used the adjective for the scriptures.

"Whoever fights monsters should see to it that in the process he does not become a monster. And when you look long into an abyss, the abyss also looks into you" (Nietzsche). I hope it is not melodramatic to think that as we fight unconventional wars, we must not become morally unconventional in a willingness to use torture, humiliation, random killings, and those other events that erupt now and again in Iraq and elsewhere.

Recent reports on interrogation "protocols" used by the CIA and others indicate how easily we can become the monsters we want to fight. Evidently, if the reports are true, we have driven people crazy.

A nice story told of the Buddha in the form of a dialogue:

> **Pilgrim**: Are you a god?
> **Buddha**: I am not a god.
> **Pilgrim**: What are you?
> **Buddha**: I am awake!

The old Irish monks had a gift for brevity. Here is the rule of life of Saint Comgall of Bangor (died 602):

> Love Christ.
> Hate wealth.
> Piety toward the King of the sun.
> Smoothness toward all men.
> Amen.

I particularly like that word "smoothness," even though today to describe someone as "smooth" is not a particular adjective of praise.

Here is a nice prayer from the Venerable Bede, useful for all theologians:

"I pray You, noble Jesus, that as You have graciously granted me joyfully to imbibe the words of Your Knowledge, so You will also of Your bounty grant me to come at length to Yourself, the Fount of all wisdom, and to dwell in Your presence forever. Amen." (This was appended to his list of works—written by him or maybe his secretary.)

———————————————■———————————————

There is a lot about Teilhard de Chardin that I am ambivalent about, but one must admire his fundamental decision never to allow his faith to become a *cassette close*—he did try to integrate his work in science and theology. I have never been sympathetic to people who easily dismiss him for this or that reason—the problem with Teilhard is that his ideas never got out into the theological marketplace where they would be critiqued. If there is any object lesson to be learned about the dangers to Catholic intellectual life coming from prior censorship, his is a textbook example. If the Roman authorities in the 1950s had allowed him to be read and discussed (I bought his books in the very late 1950s by ordering them from London or Paris, because the theological booksellers did not stock his books in Rome—they came in the proverbial "brown paper wrapping"), his ideas could have been refined. His "Mass on the World" and his *Le Milieu Divin* contain profound meditations on Colossians 1:17 and Ephesians 1:10—they can still inspire. I am also partial to his linking Eucharist and creation—a link that contains within it seminal ideas on sacramentality.

Alas, Teilhard lived in the anti-modernist world of Vatican repression and paid the price for it. That he dropped dead on the streets of New York City, in exile from Paris and the *College de France*, on Easter Sunday morning is more than poignant. That he is buried in a Jesuit cemetery on the grounds of the

New York Province's former novitiate (now owned by the
Culinary Institute of America) edges towards the grotesque.

Since I am always on the lookout for anything that has to do
with saints, maybe somewhere I can work in this line from a
poem by John Ashbery: "Now is not the/ moment to turn on a
dime or even ask what saint to pray to/given that they are all
alike, /that is, holy . . ."

Some short observations about prayer that could be given to
students or others for consideration:

"The less one prays, the worse it goes." (John Chapman)

"I do not understand your ways, but you know the way
for me." (D. Bonhoeffer)

"The power to unite myself with God's will is itself the
hearing of a prayer." (O. Cullman)

"The true relation in prayer is not when God hears what is
prayed for, but when the person praying hears what God wills.
The true man of prayer only attends." (S. Kierkegaard)

"Love is a direction and not a state of the soul." (Simone
Weil)

"Entrance into prayer is an act of faith. Prayer is simply believing that we are in the mystery of God, that we are

encompassed in that mystery, that we are really plunged into and immersed in it . . . 'In Him we live and move and have our being'" (Acts 17:28). (Henri Le Saux)

"Lord, do not abandon your unfinished work; bring to perfection all that is wanting in me." (Augustine)

"Prayer does not change God but it changes the one who prays." (S. Kierkegaard)

"If we experience God in contemplation, we experience Him not for ourselves alone but for others." (Thomas Merton)

"It is not we who choose to awaken ourselves but God who chooses to awaken us." (Thomas Merton)

"I do not know if I believe in God or not . . . but the essential thing is to put oneself in a frame of mind which is close to that of prayer." (Henri Matisse)

"We do not really see light but only lower things lit by it." (C. S. Lewis)

"Prayer should therefore be short and pure unless perhaps it is prolonged under the inspiration of grace." (*Rule of Benedict*)

"When the gods wish to punish us, they answer our prayers." (Oscar Wilde)

"God may have imposed simple prayer and obedience on some men as the instrument of their attaining to the mysteries and precepts of Christianity." (John Henry Newman)

"The peace of God which surpasses all understanding." (Phil 4:7)

"The One who is above all names has many names." (Gregory of Nyssa)

"Hurry is the death of prayer." (George Herbert)

"To clasp the hands in prayer is the beginning of the uprising against the disorders of the world." (Karl Barth)

"Everything that turns a person in the direction of God is a prayer." (Ignatius of Loyola)

"Prayer is 'wasting time' before God." (Michel Quoist)

"The wish to pray is prayer itself." (George Bernanos)

"It is better in prayer to have a heart without words than words without a heart." (Mohandas Gandhi)

"The purpose of prayer is good works." (Teresa of Avila)

"Many people reason quite the wrong way round about prayer, thinking that good action and all sorts of preliminary measures render us capable of prayer. But quite the reverse is the case: it is prayer which bears fruit in good works and all virtues." (*The Way of a Pilgrim*)

"You should not think of prayer as a matter of words but as a desire for God . . ." (John Chrysostom, *Homily on Prayer*)

"Prayer consists of attention . . ." (Simone Weil)

Three short prayers useful to say before reading scripture (from Book XI of the *Confessions*):

"Open to me the pages of your book!"

"Let me acknowledge as yours whatever I find in your books."

"Open your doors to my knocking."

A Zen master said that there are two ways to become a great painter: one is to learn the best techniques—study color forms, practice brush strokes incessantly, work under a master, etc. The other way is to become perfect and paint naturally.

One of the more useful things I studied as an undergraduate was in a class on classical rhetoric about fallacies in argument. That long ago class came back to me yesterday evening while listening to a political debate on television. As one speaker made a case for the death penalty, I kept mumbling to myself, "That is a *post hoc ergo propter hoc* argument!!"

Daniel 9 tries to puzzle out the oracles of Jeremiah; the eunuch from Ethiopia in the Acts of the Apostles tries to understand the meaning of Isaiah 53; 2 Peter warns about Pauline passages hard to understand. I must remember those loci when students complain about the difficulty of understanding the Bible. In a certain sense, the entire New Testament (or, at least, vast swaths of it) is like a long midrash wrestling with what had come before in the Hebrew scriptures.

Karl Rahner says somewhere that every preacher of the Gospel is, fundamentally, a translator; to which I would add: in two senses. The preacher must both hand over (translate) and interpret by making one language into another one.

It is clear that one can only begin to make some sense out of the Bible when it is read whole cloth. As Northrop Frye once said in *The Great Code*—the Bible is endlessly self-referential.

Among other things, the meaning of the Bible is within the Bible itself, as our liturgy makes abundantly clear; after all, we read from both testaments at every Mass—that is not an unimportant datum; we just assume it as a given. Almost nobody gives a homily exclusively on the Old Testament reading; that is a shame and a loss of a pedagogical opportunity.

While doing research for a book on Christian spirituality I compiled over twenty-five definitions of the word "spirituality"—they were later appended to the first chapter of the published work. "Spirituality," like a lot of words in my field, is notoriously hard to define, as the literature attempting to define the word "religion" attest. In the case of spirituality, it is the case that the word is used somewhat promiscuously (e.g., "I am spiritual but not religious"). However, Joann Wolski

Conn once made a very telling point in an essay she wrote for the collection *Freeing Theology*: "Definitions of spirituality may be generic but there are no generic spiritualities."

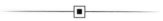

Saint Thomas Aquinas (in the *Summa* II IIae) has a discussion of courtesy that he calls variously *curialitas* and *affabilitas*. He classifies courtesy as a subset of justice and, characteristically enough, describes the vices that stand as the opposite of courtesy: flattery (*adulatio*) and quarrelsomeness (*litigium*). Both sins are punished in hell according to Dante. This piece of information came to me while working on an article on courtesy, with my attempt being to rescue the word from its narrow meaning of good manners. The invigoration of "courtesy," in its fuller sense, is a virtue much to be spoken of in an age of blowhards in the mass media.

It is nearly impossible for the theologically literate to read a passage of scripture totally free from the way a given passage has been read by the tradition over the centuries. Paul's letter to the Romans, for instance, is not a naked text when read, say, by a Lutheran or a Catholic, for the text is freighted with centuries of discussion about justification. Scriptural passages have histories. When I read the passage in 1 Corinthians about the Eucharistic celebration I have, somewhere in the back of my mind, the liturgy. It is natural, if anachronistic, for a Catholic student reading 1 Corinthians 11:23-32 to say that the text is about transubstantiation, even though that highly technical word will not enter into the Christian vocabulary for over a millennium. There is a way in which the observation of a Protestant theologian (whose name escapes me now) is right when he says that the history of Christianity is the history of biblical interpretation. Biblical interpretation, of course, ramifies out into all kinds of areas that are not technically theological. The description of the Garden of Eden, as a recent book by Alessandro Scafi shows magisterially, triggered hundreds of years of exploration, map making, etc., as attempts were made to find the garden; after all, Adam and Eve were expelled, but nowhere does the text say that the garden was destroyed. The history of cartography is deeply in debt in the West to a few lines in Genesis.

When I lived in North Florida there was an elderly gent who self-published books arguing that the original Garden of Eden was near the sleepy little town of Blountstown because a rather rare tree (the gopherwood tree) was found there and no place else (the Bible, he argued, said that Noah built the ark from such wood) and furthermore, the area was at the confluence of two major rivers, the Apalachicola and the Okloknee. I forget how he managed to account for the other two rivers. Surely he was a bit of a crank, but nonetheless, he was acting out an age-old yearning, namely, to find paradise. Judging from Scafi's book (*Mapping Paradise*) he was in very good company in his quest.

These trajectories of biblical interpretation are fascinating to follow; think of how much political theory, good and bad, has been spun out of how one goes about "rendering to Caesar and rendering to God."

I liked the distinctions made by Gerry O'Collins in his book on fundamental theology. He says that academic theology seeks understanding; practical theology looks for justice; and contemplative theology responds in adoration. Thus, theologians, honoring all of these modes, serve the ends of the Church: understanding serves community (*koinonia*); practical theology orients itself to service (*diakonia*); and contemplative theology nourishes worship (*leitourgia*). Benedict XVI uses that same triad in his inaugural encyclical *Deus Caritas Est*.

A perceptive comment by Meister Eckhart: "Since a man in this life cannot be without works, which are proper to humans, and are so many kinds, therefore he must learn to possess his God in all things and to remain unimpeded, whatever he may be doing, whatever he may be." This observation is consonant with other things that Eckhart says about the presence of God in the ordinary.

Somewhere Eckhart observes that one can live in the desert in the midst of the marketplace. It would be useful to tease out all of his observations on this theme because it is a key to the Meister's sense of re-collection. It is not unlike but not exactly the same as Brother Lawrence of the Resurrection on practicing the presence of God. One cannot constantly be explicitly conscious of the presence of God in life, but it is possible to re-collect or remember God explicitly. It is something we do, as I often tell students, when we do simple things like punctuate our day by morning prayers or a brief grace before meals. Grace before meals is one of the most important devotional practices in the spiritual tradition, and it is worthy of more serious reflection than we ordinarily give it.

Here is another observation of Eckhart on the same theme (these all come from the talks he gave young friars in the evening before Compline): "Whoever really and truly has God, has him everywhere in the street and in company with everyone, just as much as in church or in solitary places or in his cell. But if a man truly has God, and has only God, then no one can hinder him."

And two other Eckhart counsels:

"If a man were in ecstasy as Saint Paul was, and knew that some sick person needed him to give him a bowl of soup, I should think it far better if you should abandon your ecstasy out of love, and show greater love in caring for the other in his need."

"Let a man decide on one good way and persist in it, and introduce into it all ways that are good, and let him consider that he has received this way of life from God and not set off today on one way today and then tomorrow on another and let him never be afraid that in doing this he is missing anything. Because with God one cannot miss anything."

Eckhart is a highly speculative thinker over whose speculations I have cracked my brain more than once but he is also a very human and deeply serious spiritual director whose passing comments are both brilliant and nourishing.

"An ethical person: a Christian holding four aces." (Mark Twain)

"A lay person: kneels before the altar; sits below the pulpit; and puts his hand in the purse." (Cardinal Gasquet)

Ezra Pound wrote this little poem in honor of Dives, the rich man of the Gospel:

"Who am I to condemn you, O Dives/I who am so much embittered/with poverty/as you are with useless riches."

———————■———————

We are going to pay some attention, campus wide, to Pope Benedict's encyclical *Deus Caritas Est*. In preparation for a short course to be held over five Lenten Sundays, I have been casting my intellectual net widely on the subject of love (about which Cardinal Dulles had a fine essay in *First Things* not long ago). One of the sharper comments made about love is in Terry Eagleton's little book *After Theory*. Eagleton writes: "All this is why the paradigm of love is not the love of friends—what could be less demanding?—but the love of strangers. If love is not just to be an imaginary affair, a mutual mirroring of egos, it has to attend to that in the other which is deeply strange, in the sense of being fearful and recalcitrant. It is a matter of loving the 'inhuman' thing in the other which lies also at the core of ourselves. We have to love ourselves, too, in all of our squalor and recalcitrance, if love is to be more than self admiration. That is why loving others as oneself is by no means as simple as it sounds." Eagleton puts *philia* in its place by pointing to the far more demanding habit of *agape*, and in that taxonomy of love he is thinking along lines not alien to the analysis of Benedict.

Despite what Benedict says, our students equate *eros* with steamy sex. I hope to enlarge their understanding a bit by using some ideas from Jean-Luc Marion's phenomenological study of *eros* but, given their age (ah, youth!), I think they will think of sex.

———————◾———————

Among the many promises I have made to myself that I have not kept is to study the writings of Wittgenstein more carefully with respect to his spiritual (can we call it that?) search. As a person, he reminds me of Pascal, Kierkegaard, and Simone Weil—utterly serious, profound searchers; seekers of wisdom but, at the same time, tortured, unhappy, driven souls. Here, for instance is a passage from LW's notebooks from 1914 to 1916: "What do I know about God and purpose in life? I know that this world exists. That I am planted in it like my eye in its visual field. That something about it is problematic, which we call its meaning. That this meaning does not lie in it but outside it. That life is the world. That my will penetrates the world. That my will is good or evil. Therefore that good and evil are somehow connected with the meaning of the world. The meaning of life, i.e., the meaning of the world, we can call God and connect with this the comparison of God to a father. To pray is to think about the meaning of life." When I read Ray Monk's utterly splendid biography of LW, I was deeply moved by the shape of his life. Too bad I have not spent more time pondering sentences like the ones written above—I read far too much intellectual *merde*.

From his stay in the environs of the Sahara as a young man, the two things that most impressed Charles de Foucauld about Islam were adoration and hospitality. It is good to remember that the distant impulse that led him to faith was the religious example of Muslims. It led him to pray in Paris on the cusp of his return to the sacraments and cry out, "God, if you exist, make me know you."

I had to chuckle at the line attributed to Lord Acton: "There is nothing so fearsome as one lone Calvinist in possession of the truth."

(Apropos of the above: some Scottish divine was hanged in Edinburgh in 1697 for teaching that Ezra and not Moses wrote the Pentateuch.)

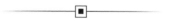

At various times I have been privileged to spend some time in the deserts of the Southwest. The desert is a basic word in the Bible, but most of us who are largely unacquainted with such geography get the impression of stark silence and forbiddingly lifeless landscapes. The Bible depicts, variously, the desert as the place where God speaks or where all forms of malignity dwell. My days in the Sonoran desert taught me first of all that the desert is anything but silent. Never mind that the shifting sand squeaks; the desert is alive with animal sounds. Coyotes yowl in the distance; javelinas crash through the paloverde shrubs at night; rabbits scurry about. Nor is it all sand; I spent a lot of time looking down at the floridly striped stones scattered about. What is true about the desert is this: it is not subject to light pollution, so if one truly wishes to experience the immensity of the sky, the desert is the place to go. It is easy to understand how the priestly account in Genesis would consider the sky above as a vast dome over the earth. The desert can also be calm. The first morning I got up for Vigils with the Cistercian sisters at Sonoita there was a small painting of frost on the ground (foolishly I did not bring a coat—hey, it is the desert) even though during the day it was comfortably warm (this was January). Of course, not all deserts are the same, but it is the case that deserts are not deserted. My experiences in the Southwest and my visits to Israel have given me an imaginative storehouse for thinking about Elijah, John the Baptist, and Jesus in relation to the desert. It almost leads me to conclude that it would be difficult not to become a contemplative in the desert.

Christian ascetics have, from the beginning, sought the desert to commune with God. One new impulse in the Middle Ages was for ascetics to create deserts as places for prayer—like the Franciscan hermitages or the Carmelite deserts—when it was no longer possible to flee to the deserts created by nature. In our own age, heroic people are drawn to the manmade deserts of urban life, and so the Little Brothers and Sisters of Jesus create contemplative dwellings in slums and *favelas* and other such outposts that stand as a sign of our own failures to care for the neediest. The demon-haunted deserts of our times are called, of course, gulags or concentration camps or inner city ghettos.

I enjoy reading the letters of Hildegard of Bingen, which are now coming out in English. One of the things that is most attractive about this extraordinary woman is her vocabulary; words like *viriditas* ("greenness") and her use of the words *symphonia* and *pigmentarius*. Hurrah for music and color in theology! John Paul II liked that word "symphonic" and probably got it from Von Balthasar.

For many years, Father Matthew Kelty said Mass at 4:00 a.m. after Vigils at the Abbey of Gethsemani. It was known as the "Milker's Mass" because it was usually attended by dairy men who are up early. On Sunday the Mass is at 6:00 a.m. and heavily attended. It is full of those tough rural Catholics who inhabit Nelson County: men in jeans and boots; handsome children with their extended farm families; older women beautiful despite the wear of years and hard work; older men hunched over in their prayers. I see the Church there in its beauty. It is on occasions like that that my faith is strengthened. We make too much of this stupid bishop or that insensitive pastor.

God knows insensitive people like that do immense harm to the Church, however. As a friend once remarked, one could put all the people who left the Church from reading a "liberal" theologian in a phone booth, but you would have to use our stadium to house those who have left the Church because of meanness, cruelty, or other failures coming from those who are officially representatives of the Church. If one were to place a compass point at the heart of Notre Dame and draw a circle out, say, to cover five miles, one would note a hospice, a drop-in center for the poor, the Saint Vincent de Paul Society, a hospital, a homeless shelter, a Catholic Worker house, a goodly number of Catholic schools, the dwelling place of many decent priests, a medical clinic for the poor, a house maintained as a respite center for those who are full-time caregivers in order to give them a day off, and a number of variously placed chapels like the one downtown to serve those who work in the area. That is where the Church is; it has a local name and local habitation. *Ubi caritas, ibi ecclesia.*

On that note: I once heard an anecdote about Karl Rahner. A university student who was a lapsed Catholic sought to regain his once solid Bavarian faith. He went to Rahner and asked for some books to read. Rahner said he didn't need books. "Go and serve the poor in Munich and your faith will be rekindled." I often give that same advice. When students begin to doubt I tell them to go to the Catholic Worker or the homeless shelter and volunteer. It is there that they will be in the company of committed Catholics who serve and pray. It is there that they will meet the true Church.

A few random citations with a brief comment:

Is it true what Peguy once said, namely, that there is not one abstract word in the Bible? It is, I think, almost totally true.

My friend Chris Nugent writes in his book *Mysticism, Death, and Dying* an observation that mysticism is like molten lava that, upon crystallizing, becomes religion. It strikes me as an observation that has truth in it but is, in itself, not totally true.

I very much like this remark of Saint Thomas Aquinas in his treatise on the Gospel of John where he comments on the utterance of the apostle Thomas who cries out "My Lord and My God!": *statim factus est Thomas bonus theologus, veram fidem*

confitendo. Thomas immediately became a good theologian by confessing the true faith.

One could write an immense tome spelling out the implication of an observation attributed to Saint Gregory of Nyssa: "Concepts create idols; only wonder understands."

Chris Nugent again: Christianity has no koans because it is itself a koan. It is replete with riddles not to be explicated but to be experienced.

The scriptural reading at the liturgy the other day was that wonderful opening of chapter fifteen of 1 Corinthians. Paul says, "I have handed down what I first received . . ." and there then follows one of the earliest creedal statements in Christianity: Christ died; he was buried; he rose again. It struck me, listening to those words I so often point out to my students, that in that small affirmation one sees the continuity of the Church. First, Paul heard; then he handed down. Nearly two thousand years later we also receive and we also hand down. Paul uses the same phrase of receiving and handing down in chapter eleven with respect to the Eucharist. At Sacred Heart basilica here on campus we listen to and enact the same creed and the same Eucharist about which Paul speaks to the little community (Jerome Murphy O'Connor thinks the Corinthian community numbered under a hundred persons).

The late Raymond Brown (at whose first Mass I was an altar boy; we went to the same high school) thought that 1 Corinthians was the text to start with when studying the New Testament. It is earlier than the gospels and provides us with a small window into the early Christian community. Obedient to his wise advice, it is that epistle with which I begin the New Testament with my freshmen students. I ask them to read through the entire epistle and make a list of every title used to describe Jesus—it is an impressive list. I like to linger over the juxtaposition of foolishness and wisdom with which the apostle opens his letter. Because our course is a survey, we cannot linger over the text for too long, but it has always tempted me to cut out a lot of other texts and just stay with 1 Corinthians on the principle of *multum in parvo*, but the temptation must be resisted simply because so often the students do not even know the basic narrative about Jesus in the gospels and that is crucial to get into their heads.

Another idea I have been tempted by but have never had the courage to put into practice: teach the students the Greek alphabet and, without any lessons in grammar, begin to puzzle out the words of Mark's gospel in Greek, picking up the grammar as we go along, but lingering over key words (Karl Rahner somewhere calls them *Urwortes*—foundational words) and explicating them at length. One could spend a lot of time just on Mark 1:1 with words like "gospel." I have never tried it, however, and my colleagues think it a crazy notion to attempt.

Why Mark? Three reasons: the Greek is simple; the book is short; and, as contemporary scholars have learned, it is a lot deeper than earlier generations thought. It is curious that none of the early fathers wrote commentaries on Mark; they evidently thought that Mark was a kind of shorthand version of Matthew and Luke. I think it is only in the fifth century that we get a commentary on Mark.

One thing is clear about Mark: the audience seemed to know the story since Mark never tells us anything about John the Baptist when he makes an abrupt entrance in the first chapter—blam! There he is. A commentator a few years back thought that the text of Mark was read aloud in its totality in early Christian communities. Not a bad idea. Some years ago, Alec Cowen had a one-man show in New York when he recited dramatically the whole of Mark on stage—it took under two hours. That was quite a feat for a modern audience, but probably also in ancient times when people were more patient, even though, as the New Testament tells, some youngster fell asleep while Paul was speaking and fell out of a window.

Choice puns:

Where there is an Oy, there is a Vey. (Robert Lax to Thomas Merton)

And a culinary pun demanding a little Latin: O Tempura! O Morels!

The papers were full of stories the last month or so about clergy embezzling monies from the parish coffers for one reason or another. One Irish-born priest serving a parish in South Florida seems to have siphoned off nearly a million dollars. It brings to mind this true observation of Saint Augustine when writing about widows: "I have, however, often observed this fact of human behavior that, with certain people, when sexuality is suppressed avarice seems to grow in its place." Augustine, as always, is shrewd, but how would he explain the priest in the Northeast who secretly garnered a lot of parish monies to lavish gifts on his boyfriend? He seems to have enjoyed both sex and money. Where would Dante put him in the circles of hell?

I do not like cheap people, like those who scrutinize bills at restaurants to figure to the penny how much of a tip to leave.

Dorothy Day was a *radical* Catholic. Here is one of her pithy observations: once we have given to God what belongs to God, there is nothing left for Caesar. There were many ways in which she put that dictum into practice. I have always loved the fact that she would not claim a tax-exempt status for the Catholic Worker. Her notion was that when you gave to the poor it should be done without getting a tax write-off in exchange. It should come from your substance (or better: the part of your substance that rightly belongs to God). I found the Day quote in a book by the then-imprisoned John Dear, S.J.

Edna O'Brien: What do you think of God?

Samuel Beckett: Nothing. Nothing. The bastard. He doesn't exist.

Ah, I think it is the word "bastard" that gives the lie to the next sentence. The proof of God is to be found in the existence of atheists!

We had an open discussion about Mel Gibson's film *The Passion of the Christ* on campus. So many people came that we had to turn away students because the fire marshal felt the aisles were impassable. The discussion was lively in the sort of way that such discussions are lively—a lot of people speaking at cross purpose and a few people getting up to orate without ever thinking of a way to shut up and sit down.

According to the newspapers, fundamentalist churches in Texas are renting entire movie multiplexes and showing the film over and over again. Gibson's scenario is based on the "revelations" of Anne Catherine Emmerich who was a purported stigmatic; her revelations were written down by the German poet-convert Clemens Brentano, and God only knows how they were gussied up via his artistic sensibility. At any rate, it is amusing to think about a bunch of Texas Baptists rapturously watching a movie based on the heated piety of Catholic devotionalism that started in the medieval period and was blown up to large proportion via baroque and rococo religious enthusiasm. I could only watch portions of the film, but it brought to my mind the more garish holy cards and bad religious art that one would find in Southern Italy some generations ago. It may have made sense in the *Mezzogiorno*, but it seems odd to think of it playing, say, in Amarillo.

So much of our faith orbits around memory—after all, central to the Eucharist is the act of *anamnesis*, and central to anamnesis is the recall of the memory of the Lord. Yet, and here dialectics come into play, we also must be willing to purify our memory as John Paul II has insisted. A purified memory then makes it possible to call up, to use the phrase of Metz, the dangerous memory of Jesus. The purification of memory plays its part in the Eucharistic anamnesis—we promise to remember and reenact with "clean hands and a pure heart." All of these ideas were buzzing about in my head after listening to a very fine paper given by Cardinal Kasper at a conference at Tantur in Israel on forgiveness and the purification of memory. Hovering in the background of his paper was the observation of Levinas that only victims can forgive. The point Levinas makes is a profound but very difficult one over which one can break one's head and, if graced, one's heart.

A point made by Kasper that requires attention: the Bible has a full theology of memory and, he added further on, it is best expressed in ritual.

A side note on above: it is possible (I have done it inexpertly) to create a profound theology out of a Eucharistic canon like the Roman one. Within it, we find ecclesiology,

Trinitarian theology, oblative theology, a full concept of the communion of saints, a theory of sacrifice, and so on. Most of all, we have, in its words, a "calling to mind . . . ," which is another way of speaking about "recollection," not as a solitary act of piety but as a collective act of in-calling the community through an exercise of memory both in word and ritual.

It was the medieval writer Bernard of Chartres who famously wrote that we are dwarves "perched on the shoulders of giants. Thus, we see more than they did and farther than they did, not because our sight is sharper and our height greater, but because they lift us into the sky and raise us up by means of their gigantic stature." It is a wonderful observation, and especially pertinent for those who study theology. It is the reason why the ancient fathers, the medievals, and others are still pertinent for us today. While it is true that there may be on occasion a paradigm shift in the doing of theology, it is also true that the roots of our theology are perennial and vibrant. It is why, to borrow a French word and an Italian one, we are always involved in *ressourcement* (going back to the sources) and *aggiornamento* (bringing up to date)—two sides of the same coin. To indulge only in the practice of *ressourcement* is to run the risk of turning theology and faith practice into a museum, while harping constantly on *aggiornamento* alone is to buy into the latest fad—a fad that soon sinks back into the memory as a romantic memory. It is the marriage of the two that strikes the correct balance. My old professor, Bernard Lonergan, could only map out the shift from classical to historical consciousness in theology—to cite one example—because he knew the sources so well. In the hands of a lesser intellect his insight would have teetered into historicism—quite a different matter altogether. In the preface to one of his books, Lonergan spoke of "reaching up to the mind of Aquinas." A classmate of mine, hearing Lonergan say this same thing at one of the English language seminars he gave on his book *Insight*, remarked to me: "If Lonergan is reaching up to Aquinas and we are reaching up to Lonergan—where the hell am I?" Well, had I the wit to say it at the time, I would have responded, "Perched on the shoulders of giants."

—————————◼—————————

Saint John of the Cross once said that God spoke his Word once and once spoken needs speak no more; we hear that Word in silence.

Here is a variation of that saying in *The Ascent of Mount Carmel* (II, 22): "By giving us, as he did, His Son, his only Word, he has, in that one Word, said everything. There is no need for any further revelation."

Over the years I have crafted a lot of talks given to wildly diverse audiences (clergy in South Florida, Cistercian sisters in Arizona, etc.) using that saying of John as a launching place.

If I had the time and the discipline, I think I could write a spiffy short book on the subject. After all, it is the same Word uttered within the Trinity, in creation, through the prophets, and in the Incarnation. Brief *dicho* but huge theme. I doubt I will ever get the energy to write such a book, but it has been on my mind for quite a long time.

Some excellent theology apropos of the Virgin Mary can be found in the writings of Saint Anselm of Canterbury; his sermon no. 52, for example, makes these parallels:

God: Father of created order—Mary: mother of recreated order.

God: Father of all things that are given life—Mary: Mother through whom all are given new life.

God: begets the Son—Mary: births the savior.

Without God's Son nothing would exist—Without Mary's Son nobody would be redeemed.

Reading the autobiography of the somewhat oddball John Cowper Powys, I ran across this thought: ". . . the mere cult of the Mother of God seems to hint at a certain element of irrational pity behind the universe, to which those of us who suffer from its judicial cruelty can turn for relief."

Right away, on reading those words, I thought of the Vladimir icon of Mary.

Watching my wife in her studio hunched over the wheel, I remembered this line from Jeremiah: "He reworked it into another vessel and it seemed good to the potter to do" (18:4). As a good husband I need to look up all those potter references in the Bible.

The Persian word *pardes,* from whence we get "paradise," is also a way to remember in Hebrew the four senses of scripture, PRDS: *Peshat* (plain); *Remaz* (hint); *Derash* (homily); *Sod* (secret). Thus: read Torah and enter paradise.

Somewhere I remember reading that Tolstoy called a "gentleman" a "left-over Christian." It is commonly asserted that Newman thought a university education ought to produce a gentleman but, some have argued, and persuasively, that the end product ought to be a saint. It is striking how much Newman wrote about saints and how often he preached about them. There is a good dissertation to be written on that topic, in tandem with his thoughts on Christian holiness of which the saint is a paradigmatic example. I have always been struck by Newman's constant theme, as early as the *Parochial and Plain Sermons*, that holiness consists of doing what one is expected to do in a faithful manner each day (or, as the old Jesuits would say: *age quod agis*). He makes clear in his lectures on university education that his *beau ideal* in this regard was Philip Neri, who spent his life in Rome taking on the ordinary exercises of the priesthood and his life as a spiritual guide day after day and year after year.

Note to myself in pursuit of this theme: Romano Guardini had very similar thoughts on the notion of sanctity in his little book on the saints and daily Christian living. In fact, he wrote that the saints of today and in the future will exhibit not the grand gesture nor the theatrical act but doing the ordinary with purity of intention and out of love. When one thinks of the dissonant culture in which we live—the easiness of our fat-laden times—one sees how prescient Guardini and others who struck the same note, in fact, are. Thus, it may be true that Saint Bertulf used to strike the sides of his iron casket (in Ghent) when the faithful came to venerate his relics but, as Butler informs us, the Huguenots "scattered his bones." Score one for the Protestants. We Catholics can probably use less of those sort of things, although the stories do hold a strange, charming power over me.

C. S. Lewis says that we need to be careful when judging purported great "saints." In his book on the Psalms he says that those who are ready to die for a cause may easily become those who are readiest to kill for it. In the same book he returns to warn us about being "great"—thus, he says that we should be glad not to be thought of as "great theologians" since one might easily mistake that for being a great Christian.

A fact about the gospels worth remembering: they never use the word "poverty," but speak of poor people ninety-five times.

Perhaps we ought to inscribe the following line over our theology building from a sermon on Ephesians by Meister Eckhart: "If you want to be without sin and perfect, you should not chatter about God."

In the airport in Omaha I saw a sign advertising the schedule of a local Episcopal church over which was this descriptive phrase: "A Band of Merrie Christians." That is a place to avoid at all costs. I have visions of upper middle-class folks dressed out in pantaloons and leather jerkins, quaffing tankards of nut-brown ale and singing carols.

A nice (and true) variation of a common prayer tag by T. S. Eliot: "Pray for us now and at the hour of our birth . . ."

While teaching in Mobile at Spring Hill College, I caught glimpses in the dining hall of television coverage of the execution day for Timothy McVeigh, the Oklahoma City bomber. How true the saying that what begins in tragedy, ends in farce: people hawking tee shirts outside the prison in Terre Haute; others peddling parking spaces on their front lawns for gawkers and reporters; a media circus as the press, like a pack of vultures, hover around filling up the hours on cable; complete idiots with "funny" placards being held up; a few bedraggled protestors. I have this feeling of being in the middle of a bad play. Thankfully, we have a huge tropical rain, complete with a lightning show, so I look at the sheets of water cascading down on the golf course behind my apartment on campus. I turn off the radio and feel blessed not to have a television set. During class one of my students, perhaps ironically, said that it was a perfect day for an execution.

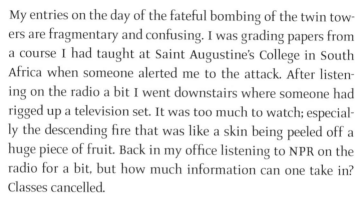

My entries on the day of the fateful bombing of the twin towers are fragmentary and confusing. I was grading papers from a course I had taught at Saint Augustine's College in South Africa when someone alerted me to the attack. After listening on the radio a bit I went downstairs where someone had rigged up a television set. It was too much to watch; especially the descending fire that was like a skin being peeled off a huge piece of fruit. Back in my office listening to NPR on the radio for a bit, but how much information can one take in? Classes cancelled.

Poet Laureate Billy Collins, when asked about poetry for solemn occasions of tragedy, replied that one could do worse than simply read the Psalms. That is what I did—from the cheesy little paperback of the NAB Psalms that is on my bookshelf. In the afternoon, Mass on the South quad with a huge crowd estimated at 7,000 persons. I stood and held the hand of a woman I know—a Melkite Christian, a native Arabic speaker, with imperfect English who was a seamstress who worked in the Notre Dame laundry—who was stricken with grief. Some months later I wrote an essay for a volume reflecting on the whole affair. Having just reread it, I realize that it was hardly up to the task assigned to us. My capacity for the banal knows no bounds.

None of our students were alive when John Kennedy was murdered. The atmosphere was quite like those days;

atmosphere is the right word—a thick collective sense of un-ease mixed with bewilderment. The incessant television coverage could become hypnotic with its continued reruns of the attack and the slow tidbits of emerging facts.

Much of the commentary lacked a strong enough vocab-ulary to make sense until they arrived at some words that rang true. There are people who are *evil* and *demonic*, and we need to use that kind of language. Terrorists are driven by an *idée fixe* without pity, love, and emotion. This is more than "insanity"—it is the incarnation of the anti-human; it is the evidence of evil in the world. I am always reminded of some-thing Flannery O'Connor once wrote; she said that when she wrote of the devil she wanted people to understand that she was speaking of the devil and not "this or that psychological tendency."

One of the iconic photos of the 9/11 tragedy was that of firemen carrying out the body of the Franciscan friar, Mychal Judge. Later I discovered a prayer he once composed with its wonderful final line:

Lord, take me where you want me to go,
Let me meet whom you want me to
meet,
Tell me what to say, and
Keep me out of your way. Amen.

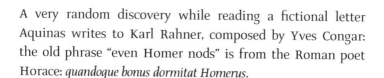

A very random discovery while reading a fictional letter
Aquinas writes to Karl Rahner, composed by Yves Congar:
the old phrase "even Homer nods" is from the Roman poet
Horace: *quandoque bonus dormitat Homerus.*

Some thoughts that could develop into aphorisms:

> The odor of incense rises up from ashes.
> Rosary beads count prayers that may or
> may not count.
> The Blessed Sacrament exposed conceals
> Christ openly.
> Martyrs die for the faith; beware those
> who kill for it.
> Candles like mystics enlighten by being
> consumed.
> Creation emerges from silence and will
> return to it.
> The most unlovable passages in the
> Bible reproach us.
> God is light radiant in the darkness.
> The deepest prayer is beyond prayer.
> Blind Bartimaeus, healed by Jesus,
> opened his eyes and saw only a man.

Hosanna in excelsis but what in
profundis?

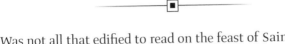

Was not all that edified to read on the feast of Saint Cuthbert
(March 20) that he would pray at night standing in water, but
two otters would dry him off as he emerged from his private
prayer so that he would be dry and presentable for the monastic office of lauds.

An Orthodox theologian (Kyriaki Fitzgerald) gave a good paper
on the Orthodox focus on Mary at a conference on Catholic
Evangelical Theology (held at Saint Olaf College). She said it
is Mary's *theocentricity* (in the *Magnificat*); her freedom (by con-
sent as opposite of Eve); her humility; her collaboration in the
divine economy; and her relationship to the Trinitarian life
in her own life. Well said, as was her additional point that as
Virgin she also exemplifies purity of heart. All of those points
could be developed at some length.

At the same conference Timothy George (of Beeson
Divinity School) made the really excellent observation that to
glory in the description of being a "New Testament Christian"
is to orbit towards Marcionism.

Every once in a while a sight jerks one out of the quotidian. In Gulfport, Florida, I saw an elderly gentleman throwing a cast net for mullet. A common enough sight in Florida. What made the scene peculiar was that he was dressed in a seersucker suit complete with shirt and tie and a porkpie hat of light blue. In addition, he was wearing those oversized sunglasses that eye surgeons give out as freebies after a cataract operation. Now, then, a poet could have done something with that scene while all I could do was to stop and wonder at it. Wordsworth made much of a daffodil; Shelley of the west wind; Heaney of a shriveled up corpse in a bog. I, on the other hand, could do nothing with the vision of the natty gentleman and his cast net. Firm conclusion: my vocation is not to be a poet.

Of Shakespeare, Ben Jonson once said that he had "little Latin, less Greek." The same could be said of myself. Nonetheless, a few years ago my Lenten resolution was to read the gospels in Greek. By the end of the season I had managed to get through all of Mark (easy Greek) and a bit of John. The most useful thing about such an exercise is that it forces one to read slowly. There is a persistent temptation to read the gospels quickly, skimming the eye over the page, because we know the story so well; at least, this is what we think. The fact is that when we read something in a different language that we know only imperfectly, we have to slow down by the very fact of that unfamiliarity. It is also striking to look at words more carefully.

Mark seems simple and naïve but as one slowly traces out the text it becomes abundantly clear that the text is far more opaque than it seems at first glance. It struck me in the opening chapter that Mark assumes that the reader/listener knows more about the *dramatis personae* than he has time or inclination to divulge. John the Baptist enters almost immediately into the narrative without introduction—he is just *there*. Furthermore, the language is redolent of crucial themes, each of which demands pondering. Mark 1:15, for example, talks about the fulfillment of time (*kairos*); the nearness of the reign of God; the need for repentance (*metanoeite*); and the imperative "believe the good news." Those simple demands at this moment of decisive time (*kairos*): repent—or convert and believe the Gospel—is the whole Christian message in a nutshell. In those fifteen verses we have already learned of prophetic voices, John the Baptist, the forty days in the desert, the quick transition into the Galilee, and the heart of the preaching of Jesus! One begins to understand why a theological commentary on Mark could fill a huge volume whereas, alas, most of the commentaries are more interested in Mark as a resource for the "search for the historical Jesus" (a noble but somewhat bootless enterprise).

———————■———————

More from the Lenten season: during this time in the Office of Readings we read through the Book of Exodus. Exodus 17 describes the battle of the Children of Israel with the Amalekites. After Moses has his arms propped up, the Israelites win the battle, and then we have the curious incident in which God tells Moses to write down a document to be recited in the ear of Joshua to the effect that the memory of Amalek will be completely blotted out from "under the heavens." The odd thing is that Amalek is not forgotten; he has been forever remembered both in the text of Exodus and in the Jewish liturgy. I only wish I was conversant enough with the Talmud to know what the sages had to say about the fact that Amalek was not forgotten, even though God said he would be blotted out. The next time I get to the library, I have got to look up his name in the Jewish encyclopedia, which is good on these sorts of things. It is similar to the fact that for two millennia we mention the name of Pontius Pilate, that two-bit Roman functionary later driven from office due to his corruption, in the Creed. It would be worthwhile to make a list of characters who gain a kind of immortality through their malfeasance. They themselves are of no particular interest but become "players" almost by an accident of history.

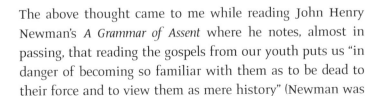

Homilists today could learn something from reading Augustine's sermons. He will frequently start a thought with the phrase, "Listen now and learn . . ." He refers to listening to the text. For Augustine, everything in the text is fraught with significance, and he will linger on this or that verse to ferret out its meaning. So often, when listening to the homilists at Mass, they are too anxious to gloss the entire reading (or even all three readings on Sunday) when it would be worthwhile to look intensely at a single verse. This is admittedly not an easy thing to do, and perhaps not even possible because of the congregation's expectation that everything is going to be wrapped up in ten minutes. Even Augustine's congregation could get impatient. In the *Enarrationes in Psalmos*, Augustine will note in passing that people's stomachs are grumbling or their patience is being tried or they are murmuring for him to wrap it up. It is those little asides taken down by Augustine's *notarius* that link us back in time to him and his audience.

The above thought came to me while reading John Henry Newman's *A Grammar of Assent* where he notes, almost in passing, that reading the gospels from our youth puts us "in danger of becoming so familiar with them as to be dead to their force and to view them as mere history" (Newman was discussing real as opposed to notional assent). Many hear the gospels today not even on the level of "mere history" but as pious tales.

It is curious, but it has only recently struck me that our imitation—as far as possible—of the virtues of the saints has a locus in something Paul wrote in Philippians 3. After denying that he had reached a state of perfection, and adding the wonderful metaphor of his pursuit to the goal as in a race, Paul adds: "Join with others in being imitators of me, brothers, and observe those who thus conduct themselves according to the model you have in us" (3:17). I heard that text read at Mass Saturday evening and it struck me then that it gives credence to my long-held notion that one of the most effective ways of leading the Christian life is to search for examples of those who have "performed" the Gospel well. Somewhere Karl Rahner wrote that the saint is the one who shows us that it is possible to be a saint in "this" way. Some saints do it by invigorating old ways of living (one could plunk Mother Teresa down in the Middle Ages and she would be doing exactly the same thing she did in Calcutta) or by thinking of new ways as, in his day, Ignatius of Loyola did. (John Baptist Metz has some good reflections on the saint as paradigm in some of his work.)

——————■——————

Going over the first encyclical of Benedict XVI (*God is Love*) has led me to think deeply about what can be that most abstract of nouns—*love*. One thing that the pope was at pains to do was to heal the purported rift between erotic love (*eros*) and the kind of love most commonly referred to in the Bible as *agape*—self-surrendering love. He takes into account those critics who have said that Christianity has destroyed *eros*, and one supposes that examples of the fear of the erotic can be found not infrequently in the Catholic tradition. What Benedict wanted to do was to put the erotic in the context of *agape*, while steering between an erotic that leads to destruction and the agapeic that moves into a destructive undervaluing of the physical, tactile, and the fleshly. It is the old polarity between angelism and bestialism about which Jacques Maritain (and later, Walker Percy in his fiction) had much to say. As part of my preparation for speaking about the encyclical, I have followed my intellectual nose down various paths, not least of which has been an engagement with Jean-Luc Marion's *The Erotic Phenomenon* where, among other things, he launches a frontal attack on the Cartesian isolation of the Ego by moving the construction of the self away from intellectualism to argue, at length, that the true construction of the human comes by asking simply this question: "Are you (am I) loved?" It is the affirmative answer to that query which grounds the *humanum*. Marion is quick to say that the erotic cannot be reduced to sexual intercourse but includes all fleshly exchange. In a sense, he eventually moves to the text in 1 John (also the inspiration of Benedict's encyclical) that God is love. What is singular about Marion's account is that in speaking of God his explanation includes the erotic in terms of his theological ruminations. Of course, like all phenomenologists, Marion does go on (and on!) like a dog worrying a bone.

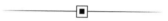

Recently there has been a spate of books that promote atheism in a militant, confrontational style (Dennett, Dawkins, Harris, et al.), often linking their objections to their faith in the total picture coming from a certain strain of evolutionary theory. I have followed this trend with a certain detachment, although my colleague down the hall (Alvin Plantinga) has entered into the fray with some gusto. On their claim (especially Harris) that religion is a positive evil to be exorcised for the sake of the future of humanity, the less said the better. But on the more theoretical issue of whether there is a God or not, I have evinced a certain curiosity, but am not overly engaged, (probably) because Michael Buckley's seminal work on the origins of modern atheism which I reviewed some years ago has pretty much persuaded me that arguments about the existence of God don't lead us very far down the path (Aquinas recognized this fact early on). I have always been taken by Newman's observation that design never persuaded him of God's existence.

Rather, because he believed in God, he believed in design. Suppose one found Aquinas absolutely persuasive relative to one of his "five ways." What would be garnered? That there was a first cause or a first mover—so what? As Buckley pointed out magisterially, once one stood on that conclusion, it was relatively easy to move beyond it, either by relativizing it or simply bracketing it. "God? I have no need of that hypothesis." Pascal was not wrong when he said, in his *Memorial*, that it is the God of Abraham, Isaac, and Jacob and not the god of the philosophers that is crucial. There is a way of thinking about all this without lapsing into some sort of crude fideism.

All of the above was triggered by something I read of Steven Weinberg's in an issue of the *Times Literary Supplement*. Weinberg, a Nobel laureate in science, is breathtakingly un-informed about matters religious proving, once again, David Tracy's comment that the one subject about which intellectuals feel free to show their ignorance is theology. (That is a judgment both on intellectuals and theologians!)

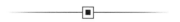

A snotty academic joke: mathematics is the second cheapest department in a university since its faculty requires only pencil, paper, and a wastebasket; cheapest is philosophy—they require no wastebasket.

Saint Thomas More said this at his trial: "Ye must understand that in things touching conscience, every true and good subject is more bound to have respect to said conscience and to his soul than to any other thing in all the world beside."

That was a powerful way of putting it—but, of course, we presume a well-formed conscience and not one, as the old moral theology books put it, working out of crass ignorance.

When, however, we operate in good conscience when our conscience is badly formed, we can be consoled by the (correct) observation of Heine: *Dieu me pardonnera; C'est son metier.*

Bob Ellsberg's book *The Saint's Guide to Happiness* has a nice discussion of the necessary distinctions between the Greek notion of *eudaimonia* (a kind of human flourishing—hard to transpose Aristotle's full meaning of the term) and the biblical "blessed" as in the Beatitudes in Matthew. Coincidentally: I have always grated my teeth every time I hear "happy" for "blessed" in, for example, the Psalms ("Happy the one . . . ," etc., in Psalm 1). I keep thinking of smiley faces. The Jerusalem Bible translates the opening of Psalm 1 as *heureux*, which is "happy," to be sure, but not in the sense we often hear it in English. "Blessed" seems so much closer to the *makarios* of the Greek. Can anyone imagine calling a Greek monk named

Makarios "Father Happy"? "Blessed" also resonates with the liturgical and familial term "blessing." My unhappiness with "happy" is a crochet of mine and I should just get over it.

I have long had the custom of reading each morning the daily entries in *Butler's Lives of the Saints* after getting the twelve-volume edition. Apart from the good information and wide range of the entries, I love the moments when the editors, in beautiful exercises of British wit, produce a judgment on some of the eccentricities and/or extreme practices of the saint. Hence for the July 27 entry on an obscure Latin American, Mary Magdalen Martinengo: when noting that as a child she decided to imitate everything she read in the lives of the saints, the editors said drily "heroic but hardly a wise program for any age." They then went on to say that they excised the examples of her personal penances recorded in earlier editions since they "would not necessarily lead to edification." Similarly, under the entry for Saint Francis of Assisi they had to admit that the saint too often appealed to cranks, eccentrics, and romantics.

Also in Butler for August 13: Saint Cassian of Imola who was stabbed to death by his pagan students wielding their styli in rage. This may all be a fiction since a somewhat similar story is found in Apuleius, but Prudentius does have a nice Latin hymn in his honor. At any rate, he could be the patron of professors, except today the students stab us with indifference.

—————————■—————————

The discipleship section of Mark's gospel is framed by two healing stories of blind people: the blind man at Bethsaida in chapter eight, and the story of blind Bartimaeus that ends chapter ten. I have often wondered, why healings of the blind? One thought that has struck me is that it may have something to do with conversion; after all, it was common in the early church to think of baptism (available only after a profession of faith) as "enlightenment" (it was common to refer to baptism as *photismos*) and, perhaps the Markan writer was thinking that discipleship (after all, this was a gospel directed to a persecuted minority) was only fully possible when one saw things in a new and radical fashion. The blind man in Jericho is described by Mark as following Jesus "on the way," and the way, of course, was the way to Jerusalem and, by extension, the cross. The theme of the "Way" is critical in Mark (it is announced by the citation of the prophet in the opening verses of the book) where, when it appears, almost never means simply a path or a road; so many translators get that wrong.

Another observation on Mark: almost nobody commented on Mark in antiquity. Probably because Mark looked like a *résumé* of the other two synoptics. Today, however, there is an intense interest in this gospel and for good reason: every time I read Mark I am more drawn into its silences and, further, by its mystery.

It is curious how, in a single day, one learns something new and gossipy and at the same time something sad and unnerving. The quotidian is interrupted by such news as, for example, today, when I learn of the firing of a difficult academic for reasons still mysterious (news enough for a chat at lunch) but also a second-hand report that a contemplative nun I know is gravely ill. The latter news hangs over my day as I try to compose in one way both my picture of this beautiful and elegant sister as I remember her and the real news that she is very, very sick. These daily intelligences are all too ready a way to remind us of the profound mystery of even the humdrum of the daily round.

A crisp observation in one of Simone Weil's notebooks: "Whoever uses the sword will die by the sword. And whoever does not use the sword (or lets it fall) will die on the cross."

And Weil again on the *Iliad* about the notion of "force": Force "that turns anybody who is subject to it into a thing. . . ."

I am not unsympathetic to Weil's loathing of the Roman Empire and its culture; much of its culture was derivative (although they did give us the arch and invented cement) and its taste for blood and violence proverbial. Gibbon may have lamented the decline of the Roman Empire, but I do not much weep for its fall.

Recently, reading some poetry of Czeslaw Milosz led me to reread some of his prose works. He became a favorite of mine after I discovered the correspondence between him (when he lived in Paris) and Thomas Merton. Milosz took the full bath in the acids of modernity and never abandoned the core of his Catholic faith. Thinking about him and his life led me to a thought that I can only put on paper for now, for if I were to express it out loud it would lead to too much consternation among the *bien pensant* Catholic coterie of today. It is this: if you were to ask me who was the greatest Slavic Catholic thinker of the twentieth century it would be, not the late lamented pope, but Milosz. John Paul II wins out for his deeply holy charisma and his impact on the world but, as a thinker, he was, by turns, constrained too much by his a priori formation and his rococo piety. That constraint shows up in his encyclicals, which manifests itself in their prolixity. It is for that reason that the best of his encyclicals (e.g., *Ut Unum Sint*) were those written largely by others. He will be remembered justly as a saint and as a public figure of larger-than-life proportions but not as a thinker. Millions turned out for the papal funeral (an extraordinary event) and few for the funeral of the poet—as it should be—but as Shelley pointed out, albeit far too exuberantly, it is the poets who are the unacknowledged legislators of the world.

As we come up to Holy Week (I am writing this entry just before Palm Sunday) we will do the full panoply of liturgical services, including a few days at the local Melkite Church. I see from a note from the basilica that I am to read at the Palm Sunday Vigil and at the 8:00 a.m. Sunday Mass on Easter morning (students do not like to get up for that "early" service). I will then go for the Byzantine liturgy with the Melkites. By Sunday afternoon I should be well exhausted, with only Easter Vespers to go. However, it is my conviction (my kids do not agree!) that one should be satiated with liturgy during Holy Week. We should be *stuffed* with the Psalms, the prophets, and the gospels during that period. Why? I am not sure, but it is a fact. The very burden of the Holy Week liturgy may help explain why in Orthodox countries, Easter is celebrated with such gusto and joy, whereas in the West we have trivialized it with chocolate bunnies and hunting for colored eggs in the backyard.

While preparing class the other day, I ran across a line that I had probably read dozens of times but had not clearly noticed; it was the cadences that struck me so powerfully this time: "So, as you received Christ Jesus the Lord, walk in him, rooted in him, and built upon him, established in the faith as you were taught, abounding in thanksgiving" (Col 2:6). The sound of those words—walk, rooted, built, established—are powerfully resonant. They would well serve as a platform for a conference, so I am going to try them out for a little talk I have to give to an undergraduate retreat at one of the residence halls next week.

Everyone knows those *mots* by which certain people both affirm and deny the hold Catholicism has on them: Graham Greene's describing himself as a "Catholic atheist" or George Santayana's credo: There is no God and Mary is His Mother. Edith Wharton had her version of this because of her aesthetic attraction to Catholicism; she said that she did not believe in God but that she did believe in his saints. Norman Mailer supposedly said (on the Notre Dame campus) that he was not sure about God but he certainly believed in the devil. Most of these are merely clever observations straining to become aphorisms, but I have long believed that they deserve some serious reflection—more reflection than I have ever given them. Of course, the greatest instance of denial but affirmation of the hold of the Catholic faith can be found in the last pages of Joyce's *A Portrait of the Artist as a Young Man.* Those pages really deserve analysis and preferably not by a literary critic. Stephen's refusal to take Holy Communion, in which he did not believe, in order to please his mother who did, would be a good place to start. Stephen did not believe in the Real Presence, but he had a feeling of awe at its symbolic weight.

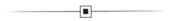

Some folks recently wrote me to ask for help in writing a "rule" for those who wish to affiliate with a monastic community. They are serious people who pray part of the Liturgy of the Hours, go to their abbey for Mass and meetings on a more or less regular basis, and now wish to formalize their practice with a "rule." I think I threw some cold water on the idea, but it was only a kindly splash. My idea is that it is far better to continue doing what they do and slowly let a "rule" (or better, some "guidelines") emerge from experience. Writing a "rule" seems to me the last thing one should do, and not the first. Why begin with a lot of stipulations that might cause anxiety and/or scrupulosity for tender souls ("Oh dear, I did not obey the Rule last week")? Practice will self-generate a "rule" or—and I like this description better—a "style of life" that is only a contemporary version of the old medieval *forma*

vitae. Too many people get enamored of the life of monks in a somewhat unrealistic fashion (egged on by self-appointed "spiritual masters" from within the community) and in their romanticism construct a pseudo-monastic style of living. Far better to learn what the monastic experience has to teach, or follow already established norms (e.g., Benedictine Oblates), rather than constructing some elaborate "Rule." On this issue I think I have history on my side.

The *Catechism of the Catholic Church* includes a very short section on the popular piety of the Catholic Church (nos. 1674-1676). In no. 1676 it quotes a long chunk of one of the final documents coming out of CELAM (Puebla, 1979) that affirms that the common piety of people (what is called, in Spanish, *religion popular*) as a kind of Christian humanism that teaches people to "encounter nature and to understand work, provides reasons for joy and humor even in the midst of a very hard life." That quotation, admittedly placed in small print, may be one of the few times (the only time?) that anything coming from the Vatican includes a nod to humor. While some popes were capable of a good quip every now and again (although it is hard to think of Pius XII saying anything funny) it is a rare enough commodity except when it is used as a kind of criticism of the Vatican itself. Romans are notorious for their biting humor at the expense of the papacy (think of the many pasquinades that tradition has given us), but humor from within in any official way is rare; perhaps its reluctance to allow for humor can be traced to the disapproval of *hilaritas* —a human tendency that the ascetic tradition always found deplorable.

A melancholy reflection on the killers at Columbine High School and Virginia Tech and their evil cousins. G. K. Chesterton once said, in one of his familiar paradoxes, that the madman is not one who has lost the use of reason but the one who has lost everything human except his reason. That paradox has the ring of truth to it. In all of the cases of mass murderers there was a careful plan of attack: guns were purchased; appropriate clothing was worn; evidence of motivation left behind. In all of this planning was the element of cool rationality. What was missing was a sense of human solidarity, a feeling of pity, an absence of seeing another as a palpable human being (hence the randomness of the shooting—that is also a random decision).

Decades ago, one of my then-colleagues (Richard Rubenstein) pointed out that after the messiness of violent outbreaks against Jews in the late 1930s (like the riots of *Kristallnacht*), the Nazis understood that such emotional lashing out would soon spend itself. What was required was a *rational* plan, and that plan was hammered out as the

"Final Solution" at the infamous conference held at Wannsee. Rubenstein saw, correctly, in my estimation, that the pure rational plan was just that—rationalized. How else to explain the clerkly demeanor of a Rudolf Eichmann, who with bookish indifference worried himself with available box cars, train schedules, use of manpower, and so on. The death-dealing at Sobibor and Auschwitz was organized along industrial lines. Rubenstein worked this all out in his still useful book *The Cunning of History*. There is something quite terrible in pure rationality divorced from humanity. History shows us that it is a constant post-enlightenment temptation: to use reason alone *sine ira et dolo* (as Weber described rationalized capitalism) to solve a problem, if that problem abuts the human person. All of this is not to say that one should exalt irrationality—there are those who live in such a condition, after all—it is to say that to isolate reason from the *humanum* is to create a lethal weapon. This becomes quite apparent when the isolated reason is put into action.

It should come as no surprise that the pope's new book *Jesus of Nazareth* should become a bestseller not only in this country, but across the world. The initial version, in German, Italian, and Polish, sold a half-million copies within a week of its appearing in bookstores. One reason for its success, in my estimation, is that it is a book fully cognizant of the critical

attitude that has been a hallmark of scholarship, especially
German scholarship, for more than a century. Ratzinger (he
writes as a private theologian and not as pope) knows that tradition well, does not fear it, and understands its limitations,
but insists that a more sapiential approach to the scriptures
is essential for the believer. In that way, he goes way beyond
lightweight debunkers (think of Bishop Spong) or the reputable (but only reputable) ideologues who fear the Gospel like,
for instance, those who tout the finds from Gnosticism and
so on. Ratzinger's book will be wholesome tonic against the
Jesus Seminar cheerleaders like John Dominic Crossan who,
as I constantly told my students and younger colleagues,
would not have any staying power as a Jesus scholar. Most
of all, the pope's book makes hash of the approach of Roger
Haight, whose approach to Christology alleges to speak to
the "postmodern" person (who might that be?) but, in truth,
speaks to an abstraction. Finally, the pope's book is a welcome
alternative to the thin gruel of the popular fundamentalists,
whose take on the Bible is not to be taken seriously, save for
those who already stand in the choir.

I usually give, to my freshmen, a last lecture or two on the
Nicene Creed, which most of them have in their memory bank
from having recited it from childhood on at Mass. My suspi-
cion is that most of them have not thought much about what

the words mean. While it takes some huffing and puffing to get them to see the epochal significance of the word *homoousios* utilized against the Arians, the more important points I underscore are these: it is organized along Trinitarian lines (deriving as it does from an earlier baptismal creed); it has diverse angles in its Christology with high and low elements; descending and ascending patterns; an articulation of the coincidence of opposites (e.g., "God from God" but "suffered under Pontius Pilate"); and so on. To know the Creed is to have an abbreviated form of the *Catechism* and, secondly, an understanding of why everyone of any note has written commentaries on it. It is one of my favorite lectures to give but it may be more a favorite of mine than it is for my long-suffering students. I give an abbreviated form of it each year when I am asked to speak to the RCIA class preparing for the Easter Vigil under the direction of the folks at Campus Ministry.

------------------------------◼------------------------------

I have been reading quite a bit of Saint Bonaventure these past weeks. Apart from his and Saint Thomas Aquinas's well-documented theological differences and their undoubted holiness (Dante makes them spokesmen for each other's founders in the *Paradiso*) how do they stack up as stylists? Well, for one thing, Bonaventure is the more lush Latinist. In his short works, he makes ample use of the *cursus*, and he often ends a section of a work with an exhortation in a somewhat homiletic style. Second, Bonaventure loves to cite the "authorities" and, especially, the more recent ones, in abundance. In a work I am currently reading (the *Soliloquium*), he provides long swatches of Bernard of Clairvaux and the Victorines.

By contrast, Thomas, especially in the *Summa*, cites with abbreviation. Thomas uses a relatively restrained Latin vocabulary and his prose is straightforward. The simplicity of his prose can beguile the reader into thinking that what Aquinas says is simple! His own voice rarely intrudes. Nor does Aquinas multiply so many points and subdivisions in his treatises. It has always amused me that the distinctions Bonaventure employs in his *Hexameron* are so complicated that the translator (de Vinck) provides a handy foldout to aid the reader in keeping everything straight. It reminds me of my old copy of Tolstoy's *War and Peace* where there is a similar foldout with the list of characters (and their patronyms) to aid the easily befuddled reader from getting hopelessly lost. I read Bonaventure most mornings with my coffee—this is not exactly *lectio*, but close to it, if one accepts coffee as part of the pious exercise of "reading."

I am going to teach a short course on Bonaventure's spiritual writings this summer, and one of the things the students will be obliged to do is to outline the day's reading (e.g., a chapter of the *Itinerarium*) with its biblical scaffolding to keep the text manageable. Fortunately, Ewert Cousins's translation makes frequent use of "sense lines"—a big help.

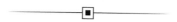

The parables of Jesus do not seem strange to us because we have heard them so often and allegorized them interminably from pulpits. To give students some sense of their strangeness, I have used some of Kafka's parables (and they are quite strange) in class. More recently I have adapted a story from Walker Percy's *Lost in the Cosmos*. Basically, I tell this story to the students: a group of people are castaway on an island, with no means to leave. There is abundant fresh water and plenty of food, the weather is temperate, everyone is in good health, the castaways get along well together, and there is little need for any work and much opportunity for frolic, including sex. One day a bottle washes up on the beach and within it is a message saying, "Do not despair. Help is coming." I then ask the students to interpret the story and react to it. Some questions might then be: Who wants to leave? Help for what? Who sent the message? Is this a religious parable? Will things on the island get out of hand? Can life in the long term be an interminable Spring Break? Does this story have something to do with religion? What happens if help does not come? Etc.

———————■———————

In reading Kevin Seasoltz's very fine book *God's Gift Giving,* he reminded me that the root of the word "decision" is a Latin verb that means to cut off or to amputate. To make a decision is, in effect, to cut off alternative choices. Obviously, this "cutting off" often operates at a very trivial level: to choose the blue shirt cuts off the choice of the yellow one just as the choice of the lamb chops means that one will not have the salmon for supper. However, at a deep existential level, to decide is analogous to convert: thus, to decide for a life of following Christ inevitably means to decide against another way of life. Thus, I see in this decision an analogue to conversion, since conversion involves an act of aversion (turning away from) just as a deep decision means the erasure of the other alternatives.

This deeper sense of "decision" adds pungency to the Gospel. When Jesus says "come follow me" one must respond with a decision: yes or no or, perhaps, later. When the young man living amid the swine of the "far away country" decides to return home to his father, his choice implicates him in a whole new set of circumstances, some from the past (repudiation of his former style of life) and some, not fully realized, about his future: how will it be at home? Seasoltz made his etymological point in passing in the midst of his very fine analysis of the nature of "gift." One sees the ramification immediately: God freely offers a gift—namely, his Son. It is of the essence of the gift that it has to be both offered *and* accepted.

In a sense, the term "gift" is common enough, but reading this book has made me alert to something: we tacitly grasp the word's meaning, but fail to recognize how rich the concept of gift really is. After all, gift is closely tied to grace in general and the theology of grace in particular. The *gift* metaphor also helps us to destabilize the too often reached metaphor of grace as some kind of spiritual liquid "poured out" on us.

A recent trip of Benedict XVI to Brazil and the papal lecture to the CELAM meeting got me to thinking about the seemingly intractable problem of the loss of Catholics to the Pentecostal sects flourishing all over the continent. One problem, of course, is that there is a huge lack of priests who are at the center of Catholic Church life (no Eucharist, no Catholic Church). Leaving aside the celibacy issue (although therein is one road to a solution), the major problem is that the priesthood is tied up with a long period of formation, the better part of which is academic. However, for the Evangelicals, anyone with a bible and a head upon which someone has laid hands needs only some folding chairs and a willing person or two who can play a musical instrument. The new lay movements are part of the Catholic solution, but the issue of the priesthood must somehow be squarely faced and, alas, is, at best, only obliquely discussed.

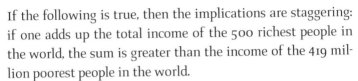

If the following is true, then the implications are staggering: if one adds up the total income of the 500 richest people in the world, the sum is greater than the income of the 419 million poorest people in the world.

Redistribution would not solve the problem, but a problem it is when one simply considers the above fact.

Someone recently wrote to me to ask whether it might be a good thing to distinguish more crisply marriage (civil contract) and matrimony (sacrament) and disengage the two. Decades ago I hazarded the opinion (in *The Catholic Experience*) gingerly that maybe we ought to think of the sacrament of matrimony (quite lately developed as a sacrament in the Tradition) as a series of stages. Let people marry civilly; if they are committed to the practice of the faith, let them marry sacramentally; when a child is born let them enter more fully into the sacrament; at a stage, make the marriage irrevocable by the "seal" of the sacrament (after which, no divorce; no dissolution via canon law). Is that an unthinkable thing? Are there resources in the tradition to even work out a hypothesis along these lines? I actually do not know—it is too far away from what I actually study.

One thing is fairly certain: from my somewhat impressionistic scan of the literature, nobody is really doing much in the way of serious theological reflection on the sacrament. I find the work of the curial courts on the "bond" inordinately legalistic; unfairly applied in various parts of the country (there are lax and severe courts) and too many people jumping through too many legal hoops. And finally, there are far too many (millions!) who are judged "irregular" in their marital status and something ought to be done about it. When the German hierarchy dipped their collective toe in these waters a decade ago, they were waved off by Rome. That may be why so many parish priests admit to me that they handle these matters in the "internal forum"—which is pastorally fine but it only serves to underscore how bad the legal machinery is. Not facing up to this fact is whistling past the graveyard.

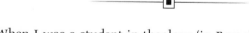

When I was a student in theology (in Rome) I read a couple of books that completely changed my life. One was Edward Schillebeeckx's *Christ the Sacrament of the Encounter with God*. It was as if the scales were removed from my eyes. It oriented me to see that the notion of sacrament as efficacious sign was not to be restricted to the seven sacraments, but was to be understood first at the cosmic level (creation is the first sacrament of God) and that Christ, as the fathers taught, was the *magnum sacramentum* and then the Church and then its signs were sacramental. I read the book in French (and still have a copy) but from it I discovered a way of tying together the whole vision of the faith. Over the years—now the decades!—I have used that notion of sacramentality in the classroom, in discussing the faith with potential converts, and, in different forms, in lectures here and there. I must confess that I was less enthusiastic with S's later work, finding his books on Jesus and on Christ very unconvincing.

The other work that changed me radically was Bernard Haring's two-volume *The Law of Christ*. I read that work in French also because my German was too poor at the time (it had to be ordered from Paris since Haring was not in good favor in Rome), but it made me see that moral theology could be approached from a more scriptural aspect—and that was a welcome relief from the standard textbooks. If I remember correctly, it was the late Josef Fuchs, S.J., who put me onto that work—Fuchs himself was the professor of moral theology at the Gregorian and a brilliant lecturer, as well as a breath of fresh air. I told one of the priests at the American College that I was reading Haring and he sniffed dismissively: "Kid, it's mysticism. It ain't moral theology." That priest later became a bishop. Of course, those were heady days for a student since we were on the cusp of the council and were ravenous for the works of Chenu, de Lubac, Congar, et al.—all the more ravenous because they were under a dark cloud across the Tiber. We had a dim view that they were mining the tradition and bringing back to light the thinking of those figures that we were getting in snippets as we worked our way through the theses of the manuals.

I have never regretted my scholastic education, however. It is so facile to dismiss the manuals but, however formulaic they were, we did learn to define carefully, to reason with some rigor, and to understand what passed for a good argument and a bad one. Furthermore, the "adversaries" were treated in historical order so I at least knew that Descartes lived before Kant and Luther before von Harnack. I still have the fat volumes produced at a prodigious rate by Bernard Lonergan over the two-year cycle as he lectured on Christology and the Trinity. They were *ad usum privatum*.

I am opposed to the death penalty for the simple reason that I can think of no person of wealth convicted of murder who has ever suffered the penalty in this country. Only the poor get the death penalty. I do believe in the penalty of life in prison. It is not a sop to my liberal sympathies to prefer life to death. In fact, think of the implications of life in prison. Never again to decide when to get up or when to go to bed. Never again to just take a drive or drop by a bookstore or eat out or stroll through a park or go swimming or walk hand-in-hand with a loved one. To have your freedom taken away for a life of regimentation which you did not choose. The saddest place I have ever visited in my life (next to a chronic ward in a state mental hospital) was the geriatric ward of a state prison. Those old-timers no longer get mail or visitors or even enjoy the camaraderie of the prison yard. They are simply in a large room smelling of piss and pine oil waiting to die and get their even narrower cell: a pine box. They end up in the prison graveyard whose head stone has not a name but a number. It occurs to me that when a "dead man walking" approaches the room to be strapped onto a gurney for his ex- ecution, there must be a part of him that feels that at least it is better than a small cell for yet another thirty or forty years. The death penalty brings a relief that the old lifers must yearn for when the call goes out to turn off the lights and they stare once again at the same ceiling of the same cell. That form of living death must be in the back of the minds of those coun- tries in Europe that want to abolish life in prison because it is cruel and unusual punishment. Maybe that is why, every now and again, I say a prayer for all those locked up for life. I learned to do that from an old Trappist lay brother who prays for them—among the many others—as he says his many rosa- ries each day.

It is for that reason the words "solitary confinement" are so ominous. Solitary by its very definition excludes one from the human community; confinement implies boundaries in its etymology. Imagine one's boundaries for life consisting of a cell that can be paced in less than ten good strides. Now, the

Carthusians embrace that life, but they do so by choice; the key word is "condemned" to solitary confinement.

We should learn to read the scriptures the way Rilke describes the reader of poetry: "He often leans back and closes his eyes over a line he has been reading again, and its meaning spreads through his blood" (*The Notebooks of Malte Laurids Brigge*). My friend the Dominican, Tom O'Meara, once described Rilke as the "permanent houseguest."

The medieval Cistercian Stephen of Sawley had an infallible cure for insomnia: he recited the Athanasian Creed. Newman loved that creed but it is wordily prolix.

"My longing for truth was a prayer in itself." (Edith Stein)

"Literature is news that stays news." (Ezra Pound)

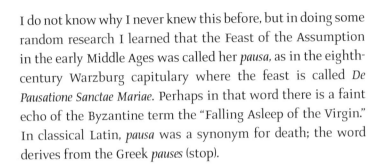

I do not know why I never knew this before, but in doing some random research I learned that the Feast of the Assumption in the early Middle Ages was called her *pausa*, as in the eighth-century Warzburg capitulary where the feast is called *De Pausatione Sanctae Mariae*. Perhaps in that word there is a faint echo of the Byzantine term the "Falling Asleep of the Virgin." In classical Latin, *pausa* was a synonym for death; the word derives from the Greek *pauses* (stop).

I have jotted down this couplet: "In the deserts of the heart/ let the healing fountain start." But I do not know who wrote it. Here is my guess: William Blake. He wrote great couplets and his lines are always memorable.

Later Addendum: I ran across those lines quoted in a novel by Ian McEwan; they are from Auden's beautiful poem on the death of Yeats.

I know that Cardinal George of Chicago gets mixed reviews at home and abroad, but one thing I really like about him is that he is interested in ideas. He comes regularly to the conferences sponsored by Lumen Christi at the University of Chicago, and I have been invited to his home (a great Victorian pile in the downtown area) for seminars, which he faithfully attends. We had such a meeting recently with a gaggle of philosophers, theologians, and humanities professors at which he was a vigorous discussant. I guess I was further struck by the fact that he participated that day soon after some serious treatment for cancer. He told me that he tired easily but one would never guess it from his participation. The topic was Benedict XVI and the question of Europe.

John Paul II beatifies and canonizes people at the drop of a hat. Many (including some in the Vatican) have complained about the slovenly way the process is being handled. There may be good reasons for this blast of saint making, but it seems to have little impact on the Catholic imagination in this country; otherwise, how does one explain the plethora of Ashleys, Madisons, Crystals, et al., that so regularly show up on my class lists? The exception to this rule seems to be my Hispanic students who carry such beautiful names as Mercedes and Lupe (for Guadalupe) and, this past semester, Monserrat (in honor of the Black Madonna near Barcelona?).

---■---

Rémi Brague, in his book *The Law of God*, wrote this about the rise of the Christian movement: "With the Church there arose, for the first time, a purely religious form of social organization with no national dimension. A society is usually founded on such natural ties as kinship, shared territory, or allegiance to a common sovereign. Here a community in which the unifying principle was not political. Judaism had already founded membership in the community with respect for the law. With Christianity, the community was founded on faith" (p. 66). I was so struck by reading that passage this morning over my coffee that I had to think for a moment about whether it was true. My tendency is to think of the Church in terms of its future: how it grew and in what direction. Now I had to think of it comparatively. The only counter-example that struck me was the development of Buddhism. It had its origin in India (but the Buddha was Nepalese) as a reform of Hinduism but spread elsewhere. The great irony is that Buddhism has a very small presence in India itself, although it can only be thought of in relationship to its Hindu (or more precisely, Upanashadic) roots. If Brague is only half-right, it is also true that this community of faith did evolve into, alas, Christendom.

———————■———————

In his sermons for the feast of Saint Francis, Saint Bonaventure will mention, in passing, that many of the teachings of Jesus, packed as they are with meaning, are extraordinarily brief. Bonaventure was commenting on "Learn from Me, for I am meek and humble of heart" (Mt 11:29). He manages to spin out two lengthy sermons on that text alone by observing that there is an introductory assertion, "Learn from Me," to signal instruction and then two words (meek and humble) that are the ways in which a disciple is instructed. Of course, the sermons are studded with catenas of scriptural passages, but the point that I took from reading these sermons is that too often when I hear sermons today, the preacher glosses over lightly all of the readings, without burrowing into a simple line. Such preachers, unlike the fathers, do not believe that much can be wringed out from little. Why should a preacher gloss over long passages and fail to tarry over a specific verse or even a fragment of a verse? If a person carries away a text (any fruitful one) it enters the memory and, one hopes, the heart. One could make a week's worth of short prayers out of a single verse or word rightly proclaimed at the liturgy. That way of dwelling on a single little verse, as Bonaventure says, means that hearers cannot be excused because they don't have books or can't remember—he was speaking, of course, to student friars at the University of Paris but the point he urges is a larger one. I must remember this when I am teaching ministry students.

Little snippets of wisdom come down to us in the oddest ways. I have never given a thought to Nicolas Malebranche since he was dismissed as an adversary in an undergraduate philosophy course decades ago. In fact, I cannot even remember why he was someone with whom my professor (or, better, the textbook from which he droned) disagreed. At any rate, Malebranche once wrote: "Attentiveness is the natural prayer of the soul." That is a very fine observation, not unconnected to the old contemplative notion of *theoria* as "gazing," and I was quite happy to learn what the old philosopher had to say. It is, however, curious how I came to learn of his observation since I would never dream of reading him. Paul Celan, that great poet, quotes the line that he had run across in an essay of Walter Benjamin, who was commenting on Kafka. I read Celan's quotation in Felstiner's wonderful study of Celan's poetry. This is a good example of "handing down," or tradition.

Frederick Nietzsche made an interesting comment about Muhammad when he said that the Prophet succeeded where Plato's philosopher king failed. For Plato, the philosopher king was only an idea that never took real form, whereas the Prophet did become the realization of the Platonic ideal. Thus Rémi Brague: "For Nietzsche, Muhammad is a Plato who succeeded." Brague goes on to say that Islamic philosophers thought that the Muslim community was the "realization of Plato's city."

From this (assuming it is true) there comes, in my estimation, a very important lesson: nobody would ever want to live in the reality of a utopia because, in my judgment, one would have to live under the authoritarian lash of one person's intellectual construct. Nobody in his right mind would want to live in Thomas More's *Utopia* for the simple reason that when such utopias are realized (think of Mao, Pol Pot, and others who tried to put Marxist constructs of utopian life into place) they turn out to be horrible. It was that aspect of the theology of hope and certain strands of liberation theology that always made me nervous. The only safe functions of utopias are to provide a distant landmark against which to hope with the simultaneous hope that they be not fully realized.

If there is one special occasion in which it is useful to observe "custody of the eyes" it is in cruising the many websites devoted to aspects of Catholicism. I feel this strongly today after spending the better part of an hour following various links about the restoration of the Tridentine rite. There are many wholesome sources of information that one can find on the Web, but it is also clear that many sites are held together by some very odd, obsessive people who, by turns, are full of spleen, unhappiness, and possessed of too vivid an imagination. What is most distressing is the vicious lack of charity—the *ad hominem* attacks on people, the careless throwing about of charges of heresy, the snide attacks, and the disdainful way they herald their own orthodoxy. It distresses me that I look at some of these sites with the avidity of those who spend the day seeking out pornography and, to extend the idea, some of this approaches intellectual pornography. It is not an insight for which I can take credit but it is a fact that this instant electronic world has radically changed the way we communicate, the way knowledge (and pseudo-knowledge) is disseminated, and the ways virtual communities are established and maintained. It is both exhilarating and bewildering.

It is very retrograde of me, but when I find a text online I print it out to read it; I do not read on the screen. There is probably a good argument against doing this, but for me, reading a computer screen is not very contemplative. You cannot walk around with the screen, underline this or that word, jot down a gloss, and so on. It strikes me that one of the reasons why our students do not read slowly and sapientially is because their eyes and minds are too accustomed to seeing everything at a glance and then scrolling down. It is hard to linger over a computer screen. Of course, as many scholars have pointed out, the page has shifted over the centuries and the way we read has radically changed (Walter Ong), so there may come a time when the use of the computer will be ordinary, and new ways of reading will develop. I sometimes feel like Lorenzo il Magnifico, who would not allow printed books in his library because he judged them vulgar fads. The volumes he had (many on display at the Laurentian library in Florence) are beautiful but were already museum pieces and *objets d'art* in the age after Gutenberg. Nonetheless, it is books I love and not electronic shadows of books. It absolutely horrified me when someone suggested I get the CD-ROM of the *Oxford English Dictionary*—one flips the pages of the OED and does not look at a computer screen.

The Notre Dame Center for Liturgy's annual conference this year is on the notion of Sunday inspired by the late John Paul II's letter *Dies Domini* of 1998. I have written a paper for the conference, utilizing the last chapter on the concept of the *Dies Dierum*. It is somewhat speculative, but it did get me thinking about how much Sunday has been wounded, not only because of the expansion of the day of rest into the "weekend" (the word was coined only in the nineteenth century as a way of describing the English gentry coming into London from their rural homes; the French, reluctantly, took over the word as *le weekend*), but also because of the rise of the stupendously oxymoronic "leisure industry." Evidently, there is a guy in our economics department studying the impact of Sunday shopping and the decline of worshippers in this country.

Here is something that has struck me: with the institution of the Saturday Vigil Mass did we also, inadvertently, attenuate Sunday's significance? I feel like a hypocrite for even mentioning the issue because for years we have attended the Vigil Mass here on campus to allow for lazy Sunday mornings of newspaper reading, messing about, and generally living the leisurely life; the latter captures the day of rest aspect, but it all seems somewhat self-indulgent.

———————■———————

In the *Summa Contra Gentiles* Thomas Aquinas has a very perceptive comment: "We do not offend God except by doing something contrary to our own good." To think out the full implications of that observation is, in essence, to sidestep the old canard that "sin" is somehow a simple matter of breaking rules or laws. It is, further, a way of seeing our lives as truly human; to seek our good in the ultimate meaning of the term is what it means to be fulfilled. It is, of course, not always easy to know what our "good" is but to seek to know that "good" is a lifelong exercise in discernment about who we are in terms of the "big picture"—always coming back from that "far country" about which Jesus speaks in his story of the Prodigal Son.

Listening to a lecture yesterday, the speaker mentioned two things in passing that are certainly worth thinking about more. First, his citation of Metz's aphorism that "Interruption (in the Metzian sense of the term) is the shortest definition of religion." And, second, Jean Danielou's warning that one should never confuse Christian hope with progress. The talk made me promise myself to go back and read a lot more of Metz (whom I met a few years ago at a conference at Tantur, where he read a scintillating paper on the meaning of Jesus in a crisis situation). Matt Ashley, my colleague across the hall, is retranslating some of Metz's work, so perhaps he can give me a reading list.

In preparing for some conferences to be given to a Benedictine monastic community, I have been reading the *Rule of Benedict* with some care. The distinguished Benedictine scholar, Sister Aquinata Böckmann, made an excellent observation about the frequency with which Benedict uses the verb "running" and its cognates. I myself am not a runner; "run only if being chased" is my mantra! Nonetheless, the image of running is a

deeply biblical one. Isaiah, for example, comforts the people
of Israel in their times of travail: "Those who wait for the
Lord shall renew their strength/they shall mount up with the
wings like eagles. They shall run and not be weary/they shall
walk and not faint" (Is 40:31). Hebrews is a nice counterpoint
text imaging Jesus as leading the pack of those who run: ". . .
let us run with perseverance the race that is set before us looking to Jesus the pioneer and perfecter of our faith . . ." (Heb
12:1-2). Of course, we have the same usage when Paul describes
himself as running. Benedict uses the verb for running four
times in the prologue to his rule and, in the very last chapter,
asks rhetorically: are you hastening (*festinas*) to your heavenly
home? Böckmann opines that the use of the term "running" is
what gives the rule its inner dynamic.

I have read the *Rule of Benedict* many times over the years
and always use portions of it when teaching the history of
spirituality. It is a wonderful text that, thanks to the work of
scholars like Böckmann (and Kardong and de Vogue and Fry),
has a profound depth that is belied by the seeming simplicity of its straightforward style. While working on this study,
I noted with some sadness that Timothy Fry died at the age
of ninety. The bilingual edition done by Timothy Fry nearly
three decades ago (with its terrific Latin indices) is a marvel-
ous resource.

How odd the peregrinations of a theologian! A week after I finished giving a retreat at a Benedictine monastery, I was in a bar in Orlando, Florida, speaking at one of those "Theology on Tap" events that are so popular around the country. Started (I think) in Chicago, groups of young Catholics meet in a friendly tavern to socialize, hear a speaker, and have a discussion about some element of the faith. I have done a number of such events. In Orlando, I was on a triangular-shaped mini-stage with a microphone and a stool. I had this weird feeling of being a standup comedian, fearful that after I made my first quip, there would be a drumroll from behind me. I have enjoyed all the times I have spoken at these events, and I suppose that it is one variation of the biblical dictum to "preach in season and out."

Here is something that I must explore. In 1 Corinthians 11:1 Paul says to the Corinthian church that they should maintain the traditions (*paradoseis*) "even as I have delivered them to you." He then goes on to speak about the relationship of women and men, including a riff on who should and should not wear head coverings when praying or engaging in prophesy. Now, in two other places Paul uses the singular *paradosis* to describe the Eucharist and belief in the Resurrection of Christ.

Question (to which I do not know the answer): is Paul making a distinction between traditions and Tradition (as Yves Congar would later use the distinction in the eponymous title of his book) or not? Is Paul distinguishing traditions of decorum in chapter 11, while later in the chapter (11:23ff) he is speaking about another kind of tradition? If there is a difference it is one that is not all that unimportant. I must query those who know more about Paul than I do.

Cormac McCarthy's apocalyptic novel *The Road* ends on a wonderful if understated note of hope after a harrowing account of a father and son traveling through a post-atomic decimated world. A few reviewers have detected the underlying religious imagery of the novel. I do not read all that much fiction but I was terribly moved by the denouement of this piece of work. It makes me want to read more of his earlier fiction.

I am weary about all the chatter from the *bien pensants* about the letter of Pope Benedict giving more flexibility to those who want a Latin Mass *a la* Trent. Who is going to celebrate such masses (most younger priests are bereft of Latin) and who will frequent them? A few out of curiosity; a few more who have never made their peace with Vatican II; and, in

Europe, at least, the old xenophobic, anti-semitic, monarchi-
cal crowd who love Le Pen and wax eloquent about *Heimat*
or *Patrie* or whatever the catch phrase is. Bah! The only long-
term good from this letter is (1) it may keep alive some sense
of liturgical continuity for a minority and thus reignite some
Latin learning; and (2) it may reconcile some of the schismatic
crowd to the Church.

Robert Alter has just published a new translation of the Psalms
attempting to keep close to the Hebrew original. The notes are
very informative, but his attempt to stick close to the compact
terseness of the Hebrew original makes it unlikely that it will
find a home for those who sing the Psalms liturgically. It is
amazing how different communities use different versions although, substantively, there are only shades of difference. A
few places chose translations purely on the grounds of musical need—for example, those who use the Grail version for its
utility in terms of the music of Father Gelineau, even when
they do not use the Gelineau music per se. Alter's introduction
is quite informative, but it is theologically toothless—not a
surprise since he is, at base, a literary critic. It was quite interesting to see Alter comment on the not insignificant number
of cruxes in the Hebrew and his best guess as to what those
puzzling texts meant.

———————————■———————————

We are seeing these days a near torrent of books written by atheists who argue the case against either religion in general or belief in God in particular. Some of these books have made it to the best-seller lists (e.g., the recent one by the execrable Christopher Hitchens) but, from my desultory thumbing through the more popular of them, it strikes me that they are not serious works. In a sense, such atheist screeds are parasitic in the sense that they presume the long tradition of Theism so much a part of our common culture. If God had died in the post-Enlightenment period, there would not be much need to exercise such vehemence in arguing against the existence of God. After all, who thunders against belief in Jupiter?

Part of the current crop of "new atheist" books is due, of course, to the baleful influence of the noisy Christian Right in this country and the truly poisonous activities of militant Islam in much of the world. It is also true, it seems to me, that the concept of "God" in so many of these works is a kind of cardboard image of God who is "up there" or "out there" managing this or that and demanding this or that. It has been one of the happier moments of my life when I began to think of God after the fashion of the late medieval mystics as *Grund*— the One who sustains all and from whom, as an inexhaustible source, everything pours forth. The noticeable trend of looking again at the picture of God supplied not only from them but from the fecund tradition of Greek patristics, insisting

on the apophatic paternity as origin of the Triune perichore-
sis and the economy of creation, has been a huge corrective
in my own thinking. Alas, this way of considering matters is
hardly reducible to a quick sound bite or a snappy response
to the village (or the media) atheist. From where will such an
apologia come? Surely not from academic tomes delivered in
leaden prose. Perhaps from the cloister or the imagination of
the poet or the sidelines of scholarship—who knows?

Yesterday I was looking through a book about art—it got me
to thinking about my favorite religious pictures. One way to
think about this is to ask: are there works of art that one never gets tired of seeing? In my case, the answer is a decided
affirmative. Every time I go to New York I try to get by the
Frick Museum to see Bellini's "The Ecstasy of Saint Francis"
(my favorite painting in all of New York). In London, my vote
goes to Caravaggio's "The Supper at Emmaus" in the National
Gallery because I am convinced that Caravaggio was deeply
influenced by the Ignatian "composition of place," which is
why he places Christ in an Italian taverna.

Last year I got back to Colmar and visited the museum
housing the "Isenheim Altarpiece." Grünewald's triptych is
stunning, not only for showing the greatest crucifixion ever
painted but for the resplendent Christ who, transfigured and
risen, stands forth in a burst of light. Finally, I love the mosaic

in the apse of Santa Maria in Trastevere for its Byzantine luminosity. It makes me want to live in Rome and go to prayer every evening with the Sant'Egidio community as they stand before that wonderful work.

Alas, I have never been to Russia, but it would be worth the trip to stand before the Rublev "Old Testament Trinity," which may be the greatest Christian painting ever. I have seen variations of it when visiting a show of Russian art in London (at the Royal Academy) and was bowled over by the subtle beauty of the variations of the Rublev original. The sense of transcendence in Rublev's work is overpowering in a way less grand than, say, the Pantocrator mosaic at Monreale (outside Palermo) which is, nonetheless, a work for which the word "great" is inadequate and which I have repeated too frequently in these paragraphs. All these thoughts came to me while reading a biography of a decidedly different painter and looking at his work: Willem de Kooning!

For a long time I toyed with the idea that a certain transcendence broke through in modern art (this notion was probably buoyed by reading too much Tillich in my younger days), but a recent long stay in front of a Rothko (an early favorite) did not satisfy in a way that "gazing" at icons satisfies. This may be a sign of getting older and more conservative, or it may be a sign that Tillich's arguments simply do not hold up over the

long run. It may be so, as he once wrote, that there is more religion in Cézanne's apples than in the art of the Nazarenes, but
that only signifies that Cézanne was the better artist. In my
estimation, Tillich simply does not hold up. I still make use of
Tillich's "Protestant Principle/Catholic Substance" typology,
but I suspect that in the long run, history will make him a
footnote in the study of modern theological aesthetics.

In the patristic and medieval world, the word "music" was very
close to the world of mathematics and, in its own odd way,
linguistics. What today we would call "music" they would call
"singing" (Latin: *cantus*). This all came to me as we sorted out
what Bonaventure had to say about numbers in his *Itinerarium*.
His ideas, by and large, are derived from both Boethius and
Augustine. Augustine (in "On Christian Doctrine") has some
interesting observations on single letters, syllables, etc., in
something very close to metrics.

It is quite impossible to accept all of what Bonaventure
has to say about numbers, except for his conviction that nu-
meracy is at the heart of reality. Music, for Bonaventure and
the medievals generally, meant proportion, harmony, order,
and so on.

At the very end of his treatise *Lignum Vitae,* Bonaventure has a really beautiful prayer asking for an outpouring of the gifts of the Holy Spirit. It is a capsule of his wonderful treatise on the Seven Gifts. A doctoral student of mine (Joan Crist) wrote a very elegant dissertation on that treatise and did a translation of the same treatise from the Latin.

I like Bonaventure a lot; having taught a short course on his writings in the summer MA program has led me to think of doing a full semester seminar using some of his more challenging texts (e.g., *De Reductione Artium in Theologiam*). That may be one of those projects to which I will never move from potency to action! Despite his tendency to subdivide everything into triads and multiple categories, he is, in places, a beautiful writer in Latin and that, in itself, is attractive.

I have been reading in fits and starts David Bentley Hart's *The Beauty of the Infinite.* It is a very powerful work of theology marred only a bit by its rococo vocabulary (he needs to read Orwell's essay on political language; it might corral his Latinate effusions), which is kind of "show-offy," and his rather impertinent judgments about other theologians and thinkers. There is a hint of the same pomposity one finds in the writings of the ever-disagreeable John Milbank. All that being said, it is a well-argued and sustained piece of theological work. I do not recall ever reading a better analysis of Anselm's *Cur Deus Homo* (although the absence of Barth's work on Anselm was curious). Hart is described as an Orthodox theologian, and it shows up in his pages on Christ—he invokes in his prose (and some of his pages on Christ are lyrically beautiful) a picture of Christ that reminds one of the great mosaics of the Pantocrator. I could not help but notice his use of Bonaventure, who would be, naturally enough, a theologian very much to his taste.

I was most especially taken with Hart's understanding of the task of theology as he outlines it in the introductory pages of his book. He sees theology as "inner witness" and *anamnesis* —a submission of language to the "form of Christ revealed in the text of scripture and in the unfolding tradition." While his work is often dense and plodding, I take it that at its core what he desires to do is to hold up for us the beauty of Christ by contrasting the *Bildung* proffered by Nietzsche with that coming from the aforementioned text of scripture and the "unfolding tradition." A wonderful strategy since Nietzsche has a powerfully expressed *Bildung* of Jesus Christ that stands in as stark a contrast to that of faith as is imaginable. Nietzsche's capacity for spleen and rancor is almost unparalleled in modern thought, at least in terms of sheer writing ability.

———————■———————

Here is a little thought experiment in which I have been engaged in preparation for a talk that I am to give: the early monks taught that what kept us back from purity of heart (through which we will see God) were the *logismoi*—the veils that darken our sight. Those eight *logismoi* became, under the influence of Gregory the Great, the "seven deadly sins" although they were more, in fact, something like illusions. Question: how would we recast those illusions into contemporary speech? Would the illusion of eternal youth, captured in our preoccupation with healthy eating and exercise and the mania for cosmetic surgery, be counted as an illusion? How about the illusion of happiness promised by advertising with the result that we possess so many things that people are making a fortune renting storage units for our overflow? How about the grand illusion of the American Way of Life as the panacea of all of the world's problems? What of the illusions of prestige, honor, advancement, and so on as the goal of the "good life"? Is the myth of the "good life" itself a prelude to illusion? Is our fear of boredom an illusion and the remedies we use to chase boredom away further proof of its illusory character? Is there not something fundamentally oxymoronic about the term "leisure industry" (Good God—one can even get a degree in it from a university!!), the encapsulation of which are many of those illusions fusing fear of boredom, consumerism, and the panting after the "good life." I am trying to sort all these out and desperately not trying to sound like some kind of amateur sociologist.

Someone this morning asked me (via an e-mail) what my main goal was as a teacher. My answer was brief: trying to instill love of learning in my students. I did not go on further to add that it is part of a larger and more subversive strategy best summed up in the title of a great classic work by the late Jean Leclercq: "The Love of Learning and the Desire for God."

Abraham Heschel on the three stages of prayer: tears followed by silence followed by song, with song being prayer. A very Hasidic observation worthy of a man who came from generations of Hasidic *rebbes*.

I found that line from Heschel while reading Ed Kaplan's new biography of him. One of the more distressing things that Kaplan tells us about is the infighting and back-biting that went on at the Jewish Theological Seminary in New York when Heschel taught there. It is far from an edifying tale; a lot of the hostility towards Heschel was motivated either by jealousy or from the intellectual disdain that some of the professors (e.g., Saul Lieberman) had for Heschel's "mysticism."

I met Kaplan a few times at Gethsemani when he was working on this book since Heschel and Merton had some ties in the 1960s.

I permit myself very small doses of the Catholic blogs—a bit of gossip from *Whispers in the Loggia*, a quick check of *First Things* to see if there are any essays of note (every now and again there is something worth reading). Of course I check out *dotCommonweal* since I contribute to their blog, and I also try to keep up with the site *Sandro Magister*. One thing that does distress me about reading some of the blogs is the readers' comments. People can be so mean spirited and poisonous when they are shielded from face-to-face exchange! There is something quite alluring for people being allowed space to express themselves in a somewhat anonymous forum. The one thing that becomes patently clear is that the world is full of very angry people who find the chance to vent somewhat palliative but only for a moment because they are soon back online ranting about this or that. Anger, the old desert dwellers said, is one of the worst of sins since it acts as an internal cancer that eats one up and fogs everything and every person that comes into the sight of the angry person. Alas, that internal fire of anger is now easily expressible via electronics. The angry, both those on the Left and the Right, appear to me to be sad and bewildered and possibly dangerous. If the religious blogs are not free from this, the political ones are even worse—more obscene and vulgar.

I recently ran across something to the effect that the Russian equivalent of the line *requiescat in pace* is "May the soil rest easily upon him/her." Is it too much of a stretch to think that the Russian saying has an implicit resurrection motif within it? Does it mean, I guess, something like this: may this person not be bound forever to the earth but, some day, enjoy the resurrection of the body?

I have been rereading Gregory of Nyssa's *Life of Moses* trying to track down an image I once found there. I often use this text in class because it so vividly shows how differently the patristic writers read scripture from the way many read today. Gregory tells the story of Moses twice; the first he describes as "history" (i.e., the sense *ad litteram*) and the second for its hidden meaning called by Gregory *theoria*. It is full of gems. When Gregory reads that Moses could only see the back of God and not God "face to face," Gregory rightly sees this as a mysterious text that requires some comment. His solution is to cite the invitation of Jesus, "Come, follow me" (Lk 18:22). Whoever follows Jesus is a disciple, and when one follows someone it is that person's back that one sees. Moses, then, will see God by following God.

Of course, it is also in the *Life of Moses* where we first get a Christian writer comparing the voice of God coming through the burning bush as an image of the virginal birth of Christ. At least, I think that it is the earliest use of that symbol, but there may be others I have not run across. Gregory makes that observation in his first telling of the life of Moses—that means, of course, that his understanding of the literal sense of scripture is far more capacious than the way we use the term today, where literal has come to mean something like "fundamentalist."

In a meditation on the Portiuncula indulgence in his work *Images of Hope,* Joseph Ratzinger makes a case for the Catholic doctrine of indulgences as well as providing a new reading of the so-called "Treasury of Merit" (I have not heard of this topic being discussed in years!). One observation he makes that is well worth noting is that if we insist on recalling only the abuse of indulgences, we have given in to a failure of memory and have fallen prey, in the process, to a certain superficiality. When I read that passing comment of the pope it was a kind of personal rebuke to me. It is so easy to resist an "inconvenient truth" by invoking the language of "abuse" so we can glide so easily over these questions: What was the tradition attempting to articulate? What insight, if any, was it urging by this or that practice? Such things can be asked when, to cite one example, we deplore an excessive form of Marian piety—let the excess not be what we look at but the impulse behind what led to the excess. This is also certainly true when we resist a "hard teaching"; I have never been intellectually convinced of the reasoning behind the prohibition (absolute!) of contraception. It always seemed to me that the reasoning for the prohibition to be an abstract edifice founded on something like biologism—but it was also true that, if one is faithful to the Church, there had to have behind it a deep truth that I could not grasp. It is surely bad faith on my part that I can avoid the issue on the grounds that I am not a moral theologian—a pathetic evasion.

Our campus museum recently had a show of the graphic work of Corita Kent. What a walk down memory lane as I looked at her splashy colors and hip religious slogans! It brought back for a time memories of those goofy years of the 1960s. Her work is very much mired in that period; they do not wear all that well. "Where have all the flowers gone . . . ?"

——————————■——————————

The Feast of the Transfiguration (I am writing on August 6) was not established in the Roman calendar until the fifteenth century; it was so entered to celebrate a victory over the Turks, which had happened on that day. How odd! The idea of the transfiguration is deeply held in Christian spirituality, especially in the Christian East where a feast day marking it has been celebrated in the East Syrian church since the fifth century. The great mosaic in the apse of the church at Saint Catherine in the Sinai represents the transfiguration and, symbolically, challenges the monks to seek for that deification—that *metamorphosis*—which is the apex of elevating (sanctifying) grace. Some of the transfiguration icons I have seen are stunningly beautiful.

It is a sad but true fact that it was on this feast day that the atomic bomb was exploded over Hiroshima in 1945. Talk about a transfiguration! Think of those bodies turned to ash. How odd that the feast day, both in its inception and due to a military decision in the twentieth century, is linked to war and, by extension, destruction. On August 9 a second atomic weapon was exploded over Nagasaki; three years earlier, on the same day, Edith Stein was sent to the gas chamber at Auschwitz; her feast day is on that date under her religious name of Teresa Benedicta of the Cross.

An idea: why isn't August 6 named a holy day in honor of the transfiguration in the universal Church as a day of prayer for peace? It would be an appropriate day to pray for personal transfiguration. Surely, Our Lady would cede the Assumption Day feast for this August commemoration.

———————————————————■———————————————————

Why is it that I cannot abide huge liturgical celebrations like opening day Mass here at the University (or even the Graduation Mass, which I always attend) or Eucharistic Congress Mass or events of that sort? For some reason they always seem to me to submerge the liturgy into a greater whole so that the *actiones liturgicae* seem diminished or set at the margins: too much liturgical swanning about for my taste. People generally love these events and find them spiritually satisfying. It is an attitude of mine that I find very hard to put my finger on; I just hope it is not theological or spiritual snobbery. Perhaps it is a resistance to worship as theater.

This thought came to me out of nowhere after watching a television clip of the end of a Tridentine Mass held somewhere in Rome. The priest was exiting, biretta clamped on his head, holding the chalice suitable veiled with the burse on top, draped in a fiddle-back chasuble, led by two altar boys with those once-standard diaphanous lace surplices. There was a time when this was the most natural thing in the world to see but now it seemed theatrical, staged—a tad robotic and not a little depressing.

———————■———————

On a whim during a recent visit I went to the Museum of Natural History in New York City, since I had not been there in years. Engulfed by youngsters thronging the dinosaur halls I began to think of Teilhard and his idea of complexification while inspecting the graphic displays showing the evolution of wings and the expansion of cranial size. It was only a passing thought, but that night I had what seemed to be an extremely long and complex dream in which I expatiated (to whom?) on Teilhard while attempting to square my thoughts on him with the biblical notion of time: beginning, trajectory, and end. I woke up in the middle of the night and thought about jotting down some of the ideas but chose sleep over writing.

In the morning I had only fragmentary notions of what my lecture was all about and no recollection to whom it was addressed. Is it a bad sign that my dreams, on occasion, are theological? Do I need to get a life? Later that day I saw a show of forty years of the sculpture of Richard Serra (at the MOMA), so why did I not give a nocturnal lecture on why I hated his sculpture so much in its coldness, over-the-top monumentality, and sheer absence of humanity? In truth, I simply said to my wife as we sat in the sculpture garden: "I hate this crap," and never gave it another thought.

———————◼———————

Reading John Piderit and Melanie Morey's long book on the crisis in Catholic higher education. What they say exhaustively is what I have observed impressionistically in my travels to various campuses around the country. The Catholic character of many schools seems to be eroding in the sense that there is a huge disconnect between the boilerplate language (e.g., a school in the Jesuit tradition or in the Catholic tradition or whatever) and the exigent reality on the ground. That a Jesuit school like Georgetown has a huge fight about keeping a crucifix in a classroom or having imams, rabbis, lady preachers, etc., in campus ministry is a direct result of the diminishing Jesuit presence on campus as well as the declining number of Catholics who enroll. If they had not had the good fortune to be in a highly desirable location they would not be a player. That is only a conspicuous example. I recently visited a school in which the Catholics in the department of theology (they prefer "religious studies") are in a minority and became highly indignant and ferociously hostile to my benign observation that all of their hires in the future (until a majority is achieved) should be Catholics and that the first courses for undergrads ought to be in Catholic theology. I do not see a long-range future for the Catholic nature of that school. Their campus ministry program: one harried priest and a few inept lay helpers. Since it is tuition driven, and as soon as Catholic parents catch on, their days are numbered. I wonder, in the next decades, how many Catholic schools will be around that are authentically Catholic. I do not think that Steubenville or Ave Maria provide the answer: too constricted, intellectually isolated, and too, well, "peculiar." And these new experiments started by the Legion of Christ or those little outposts like Christendom? Even the names are ominous. Well, the Catholic Church is a big tent and they will live as a haven for what a friend of mine calls "The Very Nervous Catholics."

It is a hopeful sign that Notre Dame—or, at least, many at Notre Dame—sees the problem and has the best shot of making something of itself. I do not think I would have said that five years ago; the signs were ominous as indifferent administrators began to make appointments based on purely secular criteria. Here, as elsewhere, disaffected Catholics create their own issues.

Note: the above was thought out (or not thought out, perhaps) on a bumpy plane ride, so that may explain the touch of dyspepsia.

The Dominican Timothy Radcliffe, writing about Advent, makes a very important point when he said that the English language had to "wait" for centuries before Shakespeare could write his works. The language had to mature and grow through the usage of everyone from peasants to preachers. Similarly, the Word could only become flesh after waiting for

God's revelation to become ready through the act of creation, the wanderings in the desert, the sharpening force of prophetic speech, and so on.

It struck me that perhaps we are also waiting as our older religious language has become flaccid (Walker Percy used the image of a well-worn poker chip), and we search for a new way of saying the old. Where will that language come from? Most likely from the experience(s) of those who must live the language in this contemporary world suspicious of our vocabulary or those who are inserted in the horrors of a ravaged culture. Here in this country, it seems to me, the problem is that of over-familiarity. Say "Jesus" and lots of folks think of some sweaty television preacher yapping and hollering or some simpering do-gooder chiding somebody. I have noticed that when I teach undergraduates, a fireproof curtain descends when they hear a certain word and they automatically think they know what one is about to say. Utter the word "sin" and the curtain goes down in anticipation of a talk about sex.

Another observation from Radcliffe: it was only in the seventeenth century that the word "charity" meant giving a donation to a poor person. In the medieval period, charity meant the way one lived.

Is that true? I must follow up his throwaway line. One clue: Saint Augustine, in his sermons, referred to his congregation as "Your Charities" (according to the Latin text). Perhaps living as a charitable person meant living under the impulse of the theological virtues.

Quite by accident, while looking for something else, I discovered that in the earliest liturgical calendars (like the one now in Wurzberg) for the Roman usage that the fifteenth of August was marked as a Marian feast, but instead of the word "assumption" they used the Latin word *pausa*. I wonder if there is any theological freight to be ascribed to that usage—it works in Latin as a near synonym for something like "interlude" or, perhaps even, "transition." I have asked a few people but so far with little light shed on the subject. I am keeping my eye out for running into Dan, our resident medieval Latin expert.

In his not-so-great book *Fallen Angels*, Harold Bloom makes a point that is not only correct but highly pertinent for anyone, like myself, who tries to teach students how to read in the theological literature: "As Kafka prophesied, our one authentic sin is impatience: that is why we are forgetting how to read. Impatience increasingly is a *visual* obsession: we want to see a thing instantly and then forget it. Deep reading is not like that; reading requires patience and remembering" (pp. 24-25). Question: where does Kafka say that? At any rate, it took me a long time to learn how to read *deeply*.

In the same work, Bloom says that for America, religion is not an opiate; it is its poetry.

Somewhere the Israeli writer Amos Oz said, apropos of his own memoir, that sometimes "facts threaten the truth." It was a sharp observation, especially useful when one reads or studies autobiography, since all autobiography is shaped by a reconstruction of events long past (and, in that sense, is radically different from a journal or a diary). There is something narrowing in an autobiography in the sense that the author attempts to create a narrative that explains how he or she got here in the present by putting together a scaffold of events, encounters, persons, and so on that points to the present moment. Hence, it is not only forgivable but necessary to omit, elide, or even avoid certain facts in order to erect the scaffolding and to point the way.

This is of interest to me since I am proposing to teach a course on spiritual autobiography in the near future. Only a dimwit reads, say, the *Confessions* or Saint Teresa's *Mi Vida* to ascertain facts. The case is even more clear in that most autobiographical of writers, Thomas Merton, whose *Seven Storey*

Mountain clouds over certain facts (some at the urging of the ecclesiastical censor) but, given that, does not the book ring true? The prime example of indifference to facts would be Chesterton's biographies of Saint Francis and Saint Thomas Aquinas—the amount of facts are rare but the insights are frequent. Chesterton himself even said that his biography of Browning got most of the facts wrong, but his reading of the poetry was spot on.

The amount of critical work on autobiography presently being done is enormous. I will try to read some of it but will make no pretense of reading it all.

One of those evening talk shows on the Fox News television channel—where everybody screams and interrupts each other—called today asking me to appear as a guest to discuss a segment on the stigmata. I graciously backed out with a legitimate excuse. I do go on television now and again (it is part of the job) but usually with unsatisfactory feelings. It takes up a lot of time, and the actual time on air is a minute or so. My favorite medium is radio; during the period of mourning for John Paul II, I was on two different shows for public radio where you got the whole hour to discuss things, answer calls from the listeners, and so on. That kind of thing has the air of authenticity about it. Even the shorter segments on public radio, when the interview is brief, one discovers that the hosts are reasonably well-read and pose intelligent questions (the same, by and large, for newspaper religion editors) but, by contrast, the television interviewers are almost always sure to ask a fatuous question.

Some observations about saints:

They give more than they receive; they give more than they have. (Bernanos)

Saints should be judged guilty until proven innocent. (Orwell)

Test saintliness by common sense. (William James)

The saints tell us that even in *this* way one can follow Christ. (Karl Rahner)

Recently, a newspaper reporter called me to ask if Saint Michael was canonized. I explained that, like the apostles and many others, the angels were accepted as "holy," and from the Greek root (*hagios*), we get both holy and saint. Many (if not most) of the saints invoked in the Church were never formally canonized since the canonical process of canonization was a late development in the Church.

I am also partial to the notion that many (multitudes!) of saints live among us, but we have constructed no liturgical services to honor them.

I am also very dubious about the speed with which the Vatican has recently proceeded in matters of beatification and canonization, since many of these processes hold up persons for whom the overwhelming number of believers have no knowledge of or interest in.

The oft commonsense observation that the new militant atheists are parasitic on belief has never better been summed up than in this nearly aphoristic observation made by the late Herbert McCabe, O.P. (in the posthumous collection *Faith Within Reason*): "So far as the kind of world we have is concerned, the atheist and the believer will expect to see exactly the same features. The only difference is that if the atheist were right, the question (i.e., the God question) would not arise—indeed the atheist would not arise" (quoted by Lucy Beckett in the *TLS*).

It is all the rage now among the "postmodern" theologians to speak of the Dionysian treatise *De Theologia Mystica*. Von Balthasar rightly points out in his splendid essay on Dionysius (in *The Glory of the Lord*) that all his works must be seen dialectically; thus the earthly hierarchy in tandem with the celestial hierarchy and, more to my point, the mystical theology in tandem with the "Names of God." Many who write on "apophatic theology" do not always keep that truth in mind; nor do those who go on about Saint John's "dark night" without seeing it in terms of the very vivid "Living Flame"—his last work. This is not to say that the recovery of apophasis is not without importance or that it cannot be considered on its own. In fact, it has been a valuable path to "thickening" our concept of God in an age of facile atheism. It is also possible to think apophatically of the mystery of Christ as does, for a conspicuous example, Saint Bonaventure in his meditation on the "Sabbath Rest" in the *Itinerarium,* where we pass into the dark rest of the Sabbath of God *via* the Gate which is Christ.

Here is an extraordinary passage I ran across from Flannery O'Connor. She wrote, "For me it is the Virgin birth, the Incarnation, the Resurrection which are the true laws of the flesh and the physical. Death, decay, destruction are the suspension of these laws" (letter to Betty Hester). Within that almost aphoristic formulation is a whole doctrine both of the Fall but also of the remedy of salvation. It is crisply articulated theology at its most profound. It is also, as one notices with the use of the word "flesh," to be as good a counter-statement to Gnosticism as one would hope to find.

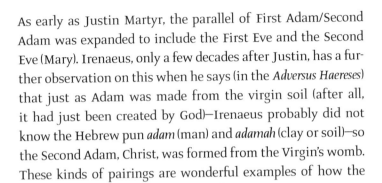

As early as Justin Martyr, the parallel of First Adam/Second Adam was expanded to include the First Eve and the Second Eve (Mary). Irenaeus, only a few decades after Justin, has a further observation on this when he says (in the *Adversus Haereses*) that just as Adam was made from the virgin soil (after all, it had just been created by God)—Irenaeus probably did not know the Hebrew pun *adam* (man) and *adamah* (clay or soil)—so the Second Adam, Christ, was formed from the Virgin's womb. These kinds of pairings are wonderful examples of how the fathers read the scriptures as a whole.

In a passing comment in his new book *Jesus of Nazareth*, Pope Benedict says that God has a special name for each person in the world. He derives this idea by a reference to Revelations 2:17. The passage itself is a bit of an enigma, but the thought expressed by the pope is a very beautiful and consoling one. It is dazzling to think that God has a particular name for me (and for you!) when we, in turn, call on God with an emphasis on our right to say *Our* Father. It is so hard to keep our concept of God from falling into some sort of abstract metaphysical concept. We need a constant reminder of our intimate connection to God, who not only sustains us but who calls us with a particular name. Thinking about that at any length leads to a discovery of what is hidden (but everywhere in scripture); in the deepest and truest sense of the word this is a path to mystical understanding.

I read recently that the film version of Philip Pullman's novel will tone down its vehement anti-Catholicism. The malign force against which the good children struggle is called, ominously, Magisterium. I know that certain quarters, like the Catholic League for Religious and Civil Rights, will be all in a huff about the novels and even the hints found in the film. Curiously enough, those spasms of anti-Catholicism never bother me all that much. What would bother me would be a total disinterest in Catholicism. It would be a sign of irrelevancy. After all: does anyone ever feel the urge to attack Unitarians? In the eighteenth century, there was much antagonistic talk about the "Enthusiasts" (a.k.a. Methodists) but who gives a tinker's dam today?

I know the hero of Sartre's *Nausea* becomes ill at his encounter with a tree, but I just had a contrary experience. Walking across campus I saw a huge copper beech tree, which I have passed numerous times. I mean *I saw it* for the first time and it struck me with wonder. I do not regularly experience such moments but, after continuing on my way, I could not but help remember that great line of Hopkins about the "dearest, deepest freshness" of things to which Hopkins gave the name *haecceitas* (their *thingness*). One wonders why one gets that "fresh eye" every once in awhile—is it a grace?—but when it happens it is worthy of being recorded because we can so casually speak of the beauty of creation. When we so speak it is often about vistas, but the true beauty of creation is to be found in its awesomely striking particularity—like a copper beech tree spreading out over a small slice of our campus. It is a shame that God did not give me a poetic gift, for that tree was eminently worthy of a good poem and too beautiful to be the subject of a bad one.

Somewhere I read the phrase "communities of memory and hope" as a shorthand description of the Church. It is a nice phrase and, brief as it is, does capture something very important. When we gather as a church we do so to remember; that is what the liturgy is all about. I have often meditated on the truth that when we gather for liturgy we stand in a long line of believers who re-call, re-present, re-enact the saving work of Jesus. That "re" in the previous sentence is connected to memory—we bring to the fore, yet again, what has been enacted. It is memory but, better, "living memory." Since we are not there yet—think of the times we articulate this in the liturgy—

we look to the future when it will no longer be necessary to remember; all will be present. That is why Vatican II puts a strong emphasis on the *eschatological* nature of the Church—it is a pilgrim community moving to a destination.

Memory is also a driving force in the encounter with sacred scripture—we look back to it not as a repository of the dead past but as a "reminder" of living reality.

I am very fascinated with the concept of memory—I always tell my students that in their daily life they should "remember" God if only by some small gestures of asking grace before they eat and begging God's blessing as they get up and go to bed. The act of remembering brings alive the presence of God in one's life.

Here are some floral motifs connected to the iconography of Our Lady that I ran across while looking for something else this morning: mystical rose, cedar of Lebanon, lily, Lady's slipper, apple (see Sg 2:3), lily of the valley, palm tree, violet, clematis, etc. There are probably many more but I had to find what I was looking for and had to resist my tendency to browse.

———————■———————

In writing about the late Graham Greene, the British critic Terry Eagleton wrote that Greene "was that most honorific of Catholics, a lapsed or unorthodox one. No club in the world is as effective as the Catholic Church in allotting honorary status to semi-outsiders."

This is true. In fact, in my youthful book *The Catholic Heritage*, I devoted a whole chapter to those outsiders. I did this because over the years I have developed an almost perfect nose for detecting strayed members of my flock. Catholic atheists in print, for example, always sound so Catholic in their rejection of transcendence. Being introduced as someone who teaches theology at Notre Dame frequently leads either to confessions of faith ("I am a Methodist but we are all going to the same place, etc.") or the lack thereof. In the latter case, I can spot the disaffected ex-Catholic in a moment. Their grievances are redolent of the old faith. I tend not to get so apologetic in those encounters for it has proved to be bootless. I do not like, on the other hand, those who try to convert me in casual conversations. Once on a plane, when someone found out about my occupation, a pamphlet was whipped out with the opening gambit: "If you accept Jesus as your personal savior you will have peace of mind." To which I responded frostily: "If I wanted peace of mind I would take Prozac." I then went back to my reading after adding that faith should not be mistaken for therapy. Religious faith should serve, at the same time, to upset and give hope.

————————————————■————————————————

In IV.2 of the *Church Dogmatics* Karl Barth reads the parable of the Prodigal Son in a way that is very strange to me. He sees the Prodigal Son as a *figura* of Christ! The Son leaves the home of the Father for a "far country," which is the country of sin and death. He returns to the Father and is welcomed in joy. What a striking reading! The only way that such a reading makes sense is to resist any attempt to make an allegory of the parable, because if one attempts allegory it is clear that the parable does not make full sense (who, for example, is the oldest son?). I wonder (but do not know) if any of the old fathers read the text in this fashion. It is, in Barth's reading, an example of the going out and coming back (*exitus/redditus*) that frames the large story of the economy of salvation.

In a discussion about this Barthian reading at lunch recently (good theology occurs frequently around a lunch table), someone suggested that the stay-at-home brother is Satan. I think not. The elder brother gains his inheritance and, as Pope Benedict points out in his *Jesus of Nazareth*, the eldest brother is a sure guarantee that we cannot fall into some sort of crude anti-Jewish supersessionism. That is quite correct and a good point to boot.

————————■————————

Someone (was it Auden?) said that one of the defining charac-
teristics of sin is that sin can be *forgiven*. Sin is never equal to
virtue, just as evil is never in an equivalent position to grace.
This is one of the most profound truths of theology; it undergirds lots of things, including hope. Let me toy around in my
head this thought: when we lose the sense of sin we also lose
the sense of forgiveness. That latter loss explains why coun-
selors and psychiatrists have such a booming business—they
might be able to palliate guilt but they cannot confer forgiveness. "Thy sins are forgiven . . ." is one of the most wonderful
lines in all of the New Testament. And apropos of the above
thought: forgiveness is at the heart of the parable of the
Prodigal Son.

————————■————————

On Halloween day, some students have been going to class
in outlandish costumes. Once when going back to my office,
I was almost run over by a student who bicycled past in a
shaggy gorilla outfit. It is amazing how we have gone in my
lifetime from a gaggle of little children going through the
neighborhood looking for treats to a mega extravaganza of
adults wearing costumes, going to parties, and so on. On television the other night, there was a report about how in parts
of Japan, people celebrate Halloween with a week of parties!

Of course, the most depressing part of this celebration is that the Christmas decorations, sales, and so on are already in the stores. Ugh!

A thought after grading twenty undergraduate papers on the Prologue of Saint John's gospel: familiarity breeds not contempt but overfamiliarity. I read about the Word, light/darkness/grace and truth/and life so often over the past morning that it is easy to become numb to how powerful those words are. So, as a refresher, I read the prologue in the Vulgate, which made me think of my youth when the priest, after giving the final blessing, would go to the left of the altar (the "Gospel side") and, more often than not, race through the prologue at lightning speed. I am not sure how the custom arose of reading the prologue at the end of Mass (note to myself: look this up), but it always seemed to me rather a bit of an anticlimax, especially since that did not end things. The priest still had to come down to the bottom step and lead the congregation in vernacular prayers for the "Conversion of Russia."

P.S. In a conversation with a visiting liturgical scholar I was told that the reading from John was introduced in the Middle Ages as an act of faith against Cathars. That sounds plausible, but still does not pin it down exactly.

――――――■――――――

My friend and colleague Nathan Mitchell has a fine essay in
Worship (November 2007) where he makes a simple but brilliant historical observation. Apropos of the drive to highlight
the "extraordinary rite" (i.e., the Tridentine Mass) many argue
that it is an attempt to get back to a more authentic liturgy.
Mitchell's point, however, is that every time in history when
the Church wishes to get to a deeper authenticity in worship,
it does not look back but does something new. Think, for example, of Pope Damasus, who wished the Romans to involve
themselves more deeply into the liturgy in the late fourth century: he had the Mass translated into Latin because Greek was
no longer intelligible (the "Kyrie" still lingers); likewise, the
Tridentine liturgy was a future-looking consolidation of the
Roman rite, not a backward look into previous liturgies.

――――――■――――――

I am reading John Richardson's third volume (of four with the
fourth yet to come) in his biography of Pablo Picasso. It is a
masterful piece of work by someone who has a vast command
of the art world in which Picasso lived. If there ever was a
sacred monster in our times, it was Picasso. He was a vol-
cano of imaginative fecundity, sexual appetites, and was one
of the twentieth century art world's more unlikable egomani-
acs. When he wrote on a painting "Yo, Picasso" it is the "Yo"

that rings out. He used and abused people (especially women) but of his genius there is no doubt. Volume three opens in 1917 with Picasso in Rome, along with Jean Cocteau. Picasso found greater joy in Naples (it reminded him of the port cities that he knew in Spain); Cocteau observed that the pope was in Rome but God was in Naples. This volume is a fat one as were the others, so I read slowly in the evenings to savor every bit of it while, at the same time, I am somewhat horrified by Picasso's egomania. He seems a person driven by some daemon that was not altogether good.

It was said that Thomas Merton looked a bit like Picasso, but it was Henry Miller who, observing a photo of Merton, once said that Merton reminded him of that "old con," Jean Genet.

Hugh of Saint Victor wrote a book called *Five Sevens* in which he set the seven deadly sins, the seven petitions of the Lord's Prayer, the seven parts of the Beatitudes (yes, there are eight, but to contain the symmetry the medieval commentators saw the eighth as a recapitulation of the seven previous ones), the seven gifts of the Holy Spirit (Isaiah 11), and the seven virtues reflected in the Beatitudes into conversation. It was a medieval handbook of spirituality. There is a critical edition in the *Sources Chretiennes* that I want to read. I came across this book in a volume of essays on the Beatitudes as read by the Christian tradition from John Chrysostom to John Paul II.

Another thought on the Beatitudes that I ran across in an essay about Bonhoeffer and John Howard Yoder (my one-time colleague), contributed by Stanley Hauerwas to a volume on the Beatitudes: much of the commentary on the Beatitudes assumes that they were uttered by Jesus as a kind of grand plan for the disciple. However, it can be argued, that they are, in another sense, a description of the meaning of Jesus himself: he is the one who mourns, exhibits purity of heart, and so on. Another way of thinking about this is to say that if we become disciples of Jesus, the very things that are "blessed" by Jesus become in our lives the realities that are praised. This is a genuine insight it seems to me and sheds additional light on the intensely Christological reading of the Sermon on the Mount found in Benedict's book on Jesus which is, by far, the longest chapter in the book.

In class we are reading the *Showings* of Julian of Norwich. As I picked up my copy, I found a ticket stub from a Notre Dame football game played in 1991 (I write this in 2007). I like to use such things as bookmarks, but especially postcards from students when they are abroad. It helps to keep memories alive. At any rate, I love reading Julian because of the freshness of her English. She uses words that had a vigor they no longer have: she describes Jesus as "homely" and "familiar"—that is, as close to us as those who gather in a family; she still uses "ghostly" for "spiritual" and so on. We know from Margery Kempe that she was sought after as a spiritual advisor but, early in her book, she tells us quite emphatically that whatever gifts she received were only for the good of all her "fellow Christians," and that whatever the Church taught was more than enough for a truly spiritual life. It is her down-to-earth tone that so attracts me. Who could not love a writer who describes Jesus as "clothing" that envelops us? So much nicer than the military dress ("put on the armor . . . ," etc.) offered us by Paul.

It is possible that Julian's frequent professions of faith in Holy Mother Church were an anodyne against any charge that she was a late follower of Wyclif, or maybe she said such things out of simple conviction or, again, as a sure way of keeping ecclesiastical censors at bay.

Towards the end of his most recent encyclical (*Spe Salvi*), Pope Benedict, almost in passing, mentions the opinion of some theologians to the effect that the purgatorial fires through which some must pass might be Christ himself. "Before his gaze," the pope writes, "all falsehood melts away. This encounter with him, as it burns us, transforms and frees us, allowing us to become truly ourselves. All that we build during our lives can prove to be mere straw, pure bluster, and it collapses . . ." (no. 47). This was a new way of thinking about purgatory that I had not really thought of before in exactly those terms, although I was familiar with the notion that the very passage of death might be, by analogy, purgatorial. The pope does not mention who these theologians are, but it is surely worth finding out. What most attracts me is how the old notion of purgatory (so odd in the way it is sometimes preached and even odder in the way it is presented in, say, art) is now re-imagined in the light of Christology and, in fact, an aspect of Christology not always emphasized: Christ as (just) Judge. All sorts of things ramify out from this central insight since the judgment of Christ is not made distinct from the saving merits of Christ on the cross. (For some odd reason, when I read this part of the encyclical, I kept thinking of Eliot and *Four Quartets*—probably because of the fire imagery, especially in "Little Gidding.")

Anent of above: while reading the encyclical in the coffee shop this morning, a colleague commented that the encyclical is too "dense" and says "nothing about Vatican II" and that "nobody will read it." I could not decide if the comments reflected a philistine mind or expressed a bit of middlebrow wisdom.

Somewhere I ran across a little anecdote about a disciple of a Taoist master. Of the master the disciple said: "He does not speak; it is sufficient enough to watch him sweep." There is a good insight in that story. I know some people here on campus who are not exactly friends of mine, but I always love to see them. The way they conduct themselves is, in itself, a kind of a lesson. The way we conduct ourselves in an ordinary way has the capacity to be exemplary. I am always telling students things like being regular in life (get to bed, get up in the morning); finding a quiet place to study and pay attention (in Simone Weil's sense of "attention"); doing what you need to do at the time you need to do it (the old Jesuit adage *age quod agis* is germane here); always recognizing and thanking staff persons; etc. What I lack, I think, is not the capacity of handing out that advice, but putting it into practice—to live in such a way that my ordinary life is exemplary. The problem is that when we try to model our lives too consciously, we come off as pompous or insincere. Here is a secret to learn: how does one go about living life unconsciously desiring ("desiring" may be too strong a word) to be a model. The ones who learn that secret are models. I need to stop giving advice and let my life be a form of instruction, without being conscious of the fact. Even thinking about this makes me feel a little pang of hypocrisy.

The Italians have a wonderful word: *sprezzatura*. It is the apparent effortlessness of an artist in full control of his or her work; it was said that Michelangelo carved marble with sprezzatura. Castiglione says in the *Courtier* that the true courtier does all things with ease—with sprezzatura. Maybe that is close to what I am talking about more generally: to live in such an unconscious fashion that others would say: that is how one should live.

After writing the above entry, I found a parallel example of how the way a person lives is as instructive as the teachings of a person. Robert Wilken (in *The Spirit of Early Christian Thought*) uses the example of Gregory the Wonderworker becoming a disciple of Origen to learn more about Christ. Wilken cites Gregory talking about the ascetic life: "He (i.e., Origen) instructed us more by what he did than by what he said."

For Advent I am reading Isaiah a bit every day in the volume of the "Church's Bible" with all the patristic glosses. The more I read, the more I love the old fathers. Yesterday, reading the glosses on Isaiah 6, the editor cites not only individual fathers

but some of the ancient anaphoras from the Eastern liturgies (like that of Saint James)—they are so lush (that is the
only word I can think of) that I began to read them out loud.
Luckily, my wife is away on a trip so talking out loud did not
identify me as an eccentric or a lunatic. They are even more
beautiful when one hears them sung aloud in the liturgy.

Critics within the Church love to attack the structure of the
current church by calling it "Constantinian" as a purported slam against the melding of church and state after the
Edict of Milan in the early fourth century. That there was
a new way in which the Church stood *vis a vis* culture after
Constantine there is no doubt, but the blame should really
be laid at the feet of the emperor Theodosius who, in AD 381,
made the Church the official religion of the state. Nonetheless
the epithet "Constantinian" has a long pedigree. In his tract *De
Consideratione* (On Consideration) Bernard of Clairvaux writes
to Pope Eugene (once a monk under Bernard's care) to excori-
ate the lavish way in which the medieval popes lived with all
of their finery, pomp, and retinue. Bernard tells Eugene that
in that respect he is not a successor of Peter but, rather, a successor of Constantine. I should copy out the whole section
where that occurs because Bernard is as vigorous and rhetorically able a Latinist as one finds in the medieval period. He
can rage with supple fury. In other places—and this is true of

most of the twelfth century Cistercians—he can weave into elegant prose hits, echoes, and allusions to Jerome's Vulgate. Great stuff!

Over the past year I have been making occasional contributions to the magazine published by our business school (the Mendoza School). The next topic will be on gluttony. I will have to try and be honest on that topic because of my own weak will when it comes to eating—there are certain foods, even though they do no good for my blood sugars, where my weakness shows through.

There is, however, one complaint about gluttony that I can make honestly, because it comes from a deep disgust and revulsion at what has become a national fad: eating contests. I can think of nothing more off-putting than to see a group of men and women shove hot dogs in their mouth in order to win a prize. Recently on television they had a program chronicling ten places in this country where one can "pig out." One young man tried to eat an enormous container of ice cream and actually threw up as he got down to the last dregs of ice cream. What is particularly obnoxious about these contests is that a few of them are now shown as "sporting events" on television. They have corporate sponsorship! In my mind there is something terribly subhuman about such activities; one could label it almost a perversion since it is beyond that kind of "pleasure" one legitimately enjoys when eating, say, in good company. In fact, the communal aspect of such contests is totally absent since the "other" is in an antagonistic position relative to the eater. Dante caught the dehumanizing aspect of gluttony well when, in the *Inferno*, he had Ciacco sitting on a mound of garbage in a torpor with eyes crossed (*strabismus*) because of the effect of his gluttony. Ciacco was depicted as an animal; hence, his nickname, the Hog (unfair to pigs since they do not in fact overeat). (The Bible, by the bye, has many unpleasant things to say about gluttony; they will be duly noted in the essay.)

In one of his vernacular sermons, speaking about how God is nameless, Meister Eckhart goes on to chide his congregation: "Be silent and do not chatter about God!" I presume it was a religious congregation he was addressing and that he was tired of useless conversation about God or useless theology being done in a superficial fashion. Somehow his warning reminded me of that line in Forster's *A Passage to India*—"poor talkative Christianity." And, it is true, that we do have a tendency to go on and on and on. Think of professional meetings of theologians. It has always bothered me to be in some overpriced hotel while all kinds of folk chat about liberation theology without noticing all of those people who are cleaning up the rooms, setting out the coffee, and so on. I am not overly sensitive but

I have always felt over-privileged when staying at good hotels, especially when on "religious" business. It is for that reason, among others, that I am not all that crazy about such events.

Recently someone wrote that the basic orientation of the *Rule of Benedict* was to develop a "culture of listening." It was not only that the *RB* begins with the imperative "Listen, my child!" but because the theme of listening not only involves listening to the Word of God but because the monks listen to the abbot; the abbot listens to the community; and the community provides space for listening to each other.

There is much to be said about paying attention to the notion of listening in the life of faith, generally speaking. In trying to develop a pedagogy of prayer, for example, listening is as important as speaking. "Be still and know that I am God" is one of the most powerful sentiments expressed in the Psalms.

Listening is also important for study. My students read too quickly (and often with earphones on). Frequently, I tell them: listen to the text.

In order to listen we need a modicum of silence—that is why, I think, Benedict wants his community to cultivate silence, although he uses, when speaking of his monks, the noun *taciturnitas* and not *silentium*. Speak when necessary and have something to say, but when it is not necessary to speak, listen.

Listening is hard to cultivate—even when alone in my office I find it hard to listen when reading or writing; the opposite of listening is not speaking—it is busyness.

This morning I was reading some student evaluations. One young man wrote very nicely of me adding, at the end, that I seemed to be like his own grandfather, "only smarter." It was the word "grandfather" that stabbed at me. There was a time when I was compared to someone's father—*tempus fugit.*

While visiting our daughters who live on the Lower East Side of New York City I could not help noticing the street names in their neighborhood: Ludlow Street, Mott Street, Christie Street, etc. Those names are in my memory because they circumscribe the haunts of Dorothy Day and the Catholic Workers. They are place markers in every issue of the *Catholic Worker*. Actually, we passed Maryhouse, which is only a few blocks from where Sarah and Julia live (right down the street from the clubhouse of the New York Hell's Angels!). One salient observation is that if this was once the home of the city's poor it is now increasingly gentrified. One still notes the bars on the Bowery ("Three shots for $10" one bar advertises!) and a few drunks wandering the streets holding beer cans in brown paper bags; one sees drug addicts line up on Saturdays for food and a needle exchange in Tompkins Square but, still and all, the signs of gentrification are everywhere: the pricy rents for apartments, the tattoo shops, vegetarian cafes, vintage clothes stores, etc. The poor will soon disappear (driven out with a certain economic tidal wave of inexorability) but to where?

One of my favorite stops in New York is to the Gotham Book Mart. Alas, it is now shuttered and closed. A few years ago it moved from its location on 47th Street (right in the heart of the diamond district) a block or so away. Now it is gone. At least the Strand is still open on 12th Street and Broadway so we have alternatives to the bland offerings of Barnes & Noble or Borders. The old bookstores are shuttering all over. I see fewer of them in London on Charing Cross Road and around the British Museum on Coptic Street (what a great name!). Sad. I love those old bookstores, especially since they seem to have been manned by people who were born to work in bookstores: sallow guys with bad complexions who dressed in Goodwill chic and knew books. They also smelled like bookstores (slightly musty with a patina of dust) and there was nary a coffee bar in sight.

---■---

This love affair with bookstores began when I was a young kid. I would bicycle down to Haslam's on Central Avenue in Saint Petersburg and look for old travel books with titles like *Through Darkest Africa with Rod and Gun*. After a good browse, it would be off to the Roxy or the LaPlaza movie house for two features and a serial. Haslams has moved further west on Central Avenue but is still in a somewhat seedy area where an occasional drunk or a hooker can be seen. Every time I go home I make a pilgrimage there to conjure up memories of my distant youth and buy a book, preferably a secondhand one.

---■---

The Bible insists that it is God alone who is holy. The root of the word in Hebrew (*kdsh*) seems to mean something like separate/different/other. Maybe it is best summed up by the old Latin tag *totaliter aliter*. That phrase is made much of in Rudolph Otto's classic book *The Idea of the Holy*. Relative to the holiness of God, everything else and everyone else takes on the character of "holy" through some connection to God's otherness. Thus, we have holy created beings, places, offices, functions, instruments, times, and so on. We humans become holy in relationship to God: "Be holy, for I, the Lord your God, am holy" (Lev 19:2). When the New Testament speaks of us as a "holy nation," it means that in Christ we are "chosen" by God as are the People of Israel. When Paul writes that the will of God for us is our sanctification (the noun in Greek has its root in the word for holy, *hagios*), he is insisting that we turn to God in our behavior and away from that which would profane us (2 Thes 4:3).

Here is a problem about which I have been thinking: how do you make attractive the word "holy" when in common parlance it is so flaccid and/or abused in our everyday speech? We speak of a "holy Joe" or a certain athletic stadium as the "holy grail" (hearing that phrase used on television is what got me thinking about this topic) or we make fun of "holy rollers." (The same problem involves the word "saint" which, again, in Greek, simply means a holy person.)

What I am trying to get across to students is that our relationship to God in whatever way we have managed to do that is an extension of holiness, which is a primordial way of speaking of God: God is holiness itself.

The late Walker Percy mused over the issue of the trivialization of religious language in both his fiction and his essays. I see it every day in the classroom. Say the word "sin" and you can see heavy mental shutters coming down at the entrance of young ears. Our religious language has become, to borrow Percy's phrase, like "worn out poker chips" rubbed down from too much usage.

Following clues in the New Testament (especially in Paul), maybe we have to talk more about seeking forgiveness, changing our lives (conversion and its opposite: aversion), responding to impulses towards God (which is what "grace" is—another tough term) as part of the *process* of holiness. We may just have to introduce the word late in order for it to have any resonance.

Some powerful texts on being prepared for God—for listening:

"Speak, Lord, for your servant is listening." (1 Sam 3:9)

The Lord called to Adam: Where are you? (Gen 3:9)

Jesus says: "Come and see." (Jn 1:38)

"He told them a parable about their need to pray always and not to lose heart." (Lk 18:1)

"Take my yoke upon you and learn from me . . ." (Mt 11:28ff)

At a conference we held on saints, Ken Woodward made the point that in the official canonization process the saint as a person is turned into a text when the saint's *positio* is written for the benefit of the perusal of the congregation dealing with the process of canonization. He did not mean that observation to be hostile or cynical because more than anything else, we know the saints through their stories. We talk about them to children, from pulpits (not enough in my judgment), in the classroom, and via art. Saints exist by and for the sake of their stories. This is a good thing. Christianity is unremittingly narrative—after all, at the liturgy, we tell a story or better, we perform a story in the very act of *anamnesis*—recalling and remembering. God created humans, Elie Wiesel once quoted from an old Hasidic quip, because God loves a good story.

The narrative quality of Christianity is a kind of triangulation (too outré to say that it is Trinitarian?)—the interweaving of God's story told in the Church through which we try to adjust our story.

The other morning it was very cold and it snowed a fair amount overnight. I went out around 5:30 a.m. to shovel our walk to save the neighborhood kids from trudging knee-deep in snow. No cars were on the road and the wind was not blowing. It is hard to discover a greater and more nourishing silence than the silence of a snow-filled early morning, punctuated only by the scraping of a snow shovel. Such silence is not exactly mystical but it does have a kind of contemplative character to it.

I went to the 10:00 a.m. Mass at the Basilica of the Sacred Heart on campus on January 20, 2008. We interrupted the Sunday schedule to celebrate a Mass in honor of the newly beatified founder of the Congregation of Holy Cross, Basile Moreau. It was the first commemoration after his beatification that took place in the early fall. I note this because long after I am gone, his feast will be celebrated at Sacred Heart, and I want to recall that I was a part of what will be a long history.

The Baptist Student Group on campus has asked me to give a talk about Catholic/Baptist relations. I know and have known extremely devoted and learned Baptists over the years, and have often been shamed by their love of the word of God. It would be absolutely ridiculous to share with them my early memories of (almost entirely) Southern Baptists who were, in the main, staunch anti-Catholics (I have memories of anti-Kennedy homilies preached from Baptist pulpits) and my distaste for those toothsome Baptist preachers in fancy suits and slicked-down hair. What saved me from being an anti-Baptist bigot was some acquaintance with heroic figures like Will Campbell and the Koinonia community who were *radical* Christians. Maybe when I meet the students I will speak of the Koinonia community (I spent a weekend with them years ago) and tell a few Will Campbell stories. Or maybe: talk about an old retired carpenter I knew in Wakulla County who drove every Sunday up to Georgia to worship with his fellow Primitive Baptists who sang simple hymns with no musical accompaniment and were the "foot washing" kind. I loved their austerity even though they were drenched in the worst kind of Calvinist predestination ideas. Better yet: maybe I will speak for ten minutes and then answer questions.

I also have to give a Lenten reflection to the liturgical choir members in a few weeks. That will not be hard to do. I am going back to notes I made when I gave the retreat to the Benedictine monks in New Jersey and still did not get said everything that could be said about the "heart." After all, none of us are totally pure of heart, and in that phrase we can also think a bit about another great theme: desire. What are the ways in which we can desire "purity of heart"? And: do we really want to desire it? It is a fearsome longing when we think about it. This has all been on my mind because a freshman student asked in class about God "hardening the heart" of pharaoh (in Exodus). She thought it "unfair of God" to do so.

Saint Blaise Day fell on a Sunday this year so I lined up, in futility as it turns out, to have my throat blessed by one of the five priests who had stations around the sanctuary after Mass. I say "in futility" because the crowds were so large and the lines so erratic (chaotic!) that I had to leave before getting anywhere close to the priest.

How odd that Catholics swamp the Church for such rites! Ash Wednesday is a magnet for people (many not Catholic) coming for the imposition of ashes, and every Palm Sunday people leave church with fists full of palms to take home.

It would be nice to think of these "sacramentals" as a cultural leftover from a simpler day but, *soi-disant* sophisticate as I may be, I love these little rites as much as holy water, the smell of incense, and all of the other epiphenomena of popular Catholicism. In fact, I think it would be a great thing to multiply these gestures—they are "binders" to the life of faith and should never be underestimated. I have actually toyed with the idea of finding a brown scapular and wearing it—after all, it would tie me back to my youth!

If I were the rector of Saint Patrick's Cathedral in New York City (which I am not), I would have someone (brothers or sisters or lay ministers) at every aisle passing out holy cards and offering to bless people with a prayer. Instead, they have surly ushers moving people along. What a wasted opportunity. Our tradition has hundreds of little things that link people, however tenuously, to the tradition and we should take full advantage of it. (I would also shut down the tacky "gift" shop and/or replace it with something more wholesome.)

P.S. I felt a bit bad all day (but, gratefully, not with a sore throat) because I did not get a blessing in honor of Saint Blaise.

Tracking down something on the Internet I ran across one of those reactionary screeds by a self-described "orthodox" Catholic lambasting somebody for doctrinal deviation apropos of a point that struck me as somewhat minor. There is so much of that kind of stuff out there on the Web and so much of it in print. There is a lady who has a website who constantly updates us on her prayer life; her little oratory at home; her search for the right mantilla to cover her head—she is the very model of a pious Catholic until she speaks of politics at which time her tongue is tipped with venom and scorn. What is disconcerting is the poisonous tone of such criticism and the near total absence of anything approaching charity or the willingness to concede another's good will. Of such persons I am in mind of a sharp comment made by Sainte-Beuve about Montaigne: he would have made an exemplary Catholic if only he had been a Christian. I think I first ran across that *mot* in a book or essay on Montaigne.

Somewhere the excellent Anglican scholar Ephraim Radner
suggested that Christians look for symbols in nature and at-
tach to them a Christian reading. Of course, there is much
in the tradition that recommends that procedure, but we do
not do it as much these days. There is no good reason why. It
strikes me that such a way of looking at nature (Hopkins was
brilliant in doing that) would be a very good catechetical tool,
especially for young people. It would be a way of recapturing
a sacramental view of creation. It would be crucial, of course,
not to sentimentalize nature. It should involve specifics as did
Francis in the "Canticle of Brother Sun." As I once said somewhere in print: Francis never talked about nature; he had an
eye for specifics: sun, moon, water, flowers, fire, and so on. His
vision was not "natural"—it was sacramental. Chesterton in
his book on Francis made the very same point. It is far from
a bad one.

Yesterday (Sunday) was bitterly cold, made all the more bit-
ter by lots of wind; the wind chill was minus twenty degrees.
Since I had gone to Mass on Saturday, I hunkered down in the
family room, built a fire in the fireplace, and read and correct-
ed papers without ever venturing out. By the end of the day, I
was restless enough to go outside for a bit to shovel the snow

from our sidewalk. Moral of the story: I would not do well in a Carthusian cell or in solitary confinement. The monks may sing "O Beata Solitudo," but my taste for enclosed solitude is limited due to my restlessness.

We had forty or so bishops here for a conference on scriptural preaching (I made a modest contribution as one of the readers of papers). I took a day and a half off from teaching to get to most of the talks. It all seemed to go well, but what was most interesting to me was to speak at the informal breaks with a number of the bishops. Here is a general impression: it is very tough being a bishop in these days; their workload is crushing; their flock restless; their clergy overworked. I am sure that it is the case that certain careerists still angle for the episcopacy, but from my distant perspective I judge that those driven by ambition do not know what they are getting themselves into. They will do a lot of penance for their ambition!

Doing my Lenten reading of John, it is striking to see how, in a single verse, John will use some of his distinctive vocabulary about which one could erect long reflections. In the Cana episode, John finishes by noting, "This first sign Jesus did in Cana of Galilee and showed forth his glory and his disciples

believed in him" (Jn 2:11). One could spend a lot of time pars-
ing "sign" and "manifested" and "glory" and "disciples" and
"believed." No wonder the fathers could linger over verses and
words with such care and at such leisure. I have read that
verse innumerable times but reading it in Greek (my Lenten
discipline) makes one slow down and ponder.

Bruce Marshall, in a wonderful paper on Aquinas as a scriptural theologian (read to the bishops at the 2008 "Eloquence
of Preaching" conference we held), abbreviates some remarks
Aquinas made about the Virgin Mary in his *Sermon-Conferences
of St. Thomas Aquinas on the Apostles' Creed.* I will abbreviate
them even more because they make a perfect little catechesis
on Mary:

>In the generation of the Word of God
>from her very self:
>The Virgin first heard;
>She then consented by faith;
>So kept and carried the Word in her
>womb;
>She brought forth the Word;
>Finally, she nourished and nursed the
>Word.
>
>Beautiful and profound!

——————————■——————————

I was struck this morning by a single line in John's gospel: "The light came into the world but men (*anthropoi*) loved the darkness more than the light . . ." (Jn 3:19). It would be possible, again, to elongate a very dense meditation on this fragmentary sentence. It is typical John language: light/darkness/world. It is a profoundly anthropological observation applicable to everyday light as it is recorded in the daily news. People lash out at people; they use them badly; they are ready for violence and war; they hurt the innocent. When we read about such behavior, we almost instinctively say: "Can't they *see* that this is stupid, senseless, and degrading?" Actors in such affairs may glimpse the stupidity of it all, but they operate in the dark with no perception of the light. The point is that often we do not see because we don't have—what?—the wit, the time, the reflection to recognize how stupid and degrading our own actions are. We do not *see*—we thrash around in the darkness. That is why John finishes that sentence by saying that the darkness of which he speaks is our evil deeds (*ponera erga* might be better translated: our "obscene deeds").

(This was a little exercise in what Karl Barth once said we ought to do: read the Bible with one hand and hold the newspaper in the other.)

Why does John in his gospel always say "answered and said" or "replied and said" when it would be more economical to say simply "he replied" or "he said"? I must ask one of my New Testament colleagues about this. Is this a Semitic usage or a rhetorical trick or what?

Rereading for class the late John Paul II's encyclical on the Eucharist. He has some invigorating reflections on the Eucharist as sacrifice (a theme often undernourished in contemporary writing on the Eucharist). I read some of those reflections in class to my students with the precise aim of reminding them (mainly the more activist-prone MDiv students) that there is more than a meal going on at the Eucharist. I did not have them engage the whole encyclical, mainly because of the late pope's prolixity—as I read the entire thing I could not always see where some of his excursions were headed; the encyclical has too many sub-themes, and they detract from its beauty.

Apropos of the Eucharist: The Eastern Church has no tradition of prayer before the exposed Eucharist or the equivalent of Forty Hours or Corpus Christi celebrations. They obviously believe in the Real Presence (as the liturgy makes patently clear) but they seem not to have a "theory" about *how* Christ is present in the Eucharist. It takes such a "theory" (transubstantiation) to have such Eucharistic devotional practices develop. Conversely: we, in the West, have no strong "theory" of icons in the way the East does—hence the enhanced devotional role of icons in the East.

David Hume referred to the scholarly life as the "sedentary profession," a phrase he did not mean to be ironic. It is an aptly economical description for both professors and their graduate students who need to learn the iron discipline of sitting at the desk with nose in book. Unless one learns to do that, academic study is drudgery. Let the *bien pensants* scorn the ivory tower, but I am happiest when I arrive at the office and *sit down* at my desk. The very fact that I have a desk and an office to keep books and papers is in its own right a great boon. Furthermore, even though we do lots of valuable things as a community (e.g., at a good seminar) and enjoy setting out to speak here or visit there, the brute fact is that the only way to become a scholar and to love its life is to sit down and study as a solitary act. Until one does that, he or she has no right to prattle on before folks without having first studied. The psalmist gets it right in the opening of the Psalter: "their delight is in the law of the Lord and on his law they meditate day and night"—that is the counterpoint to those who "sit in the seat of the scoffers." The wise man knows where to plant his bottom!

While planning to give a Lenten reflection to the campus liturgical choir, I keep going back to the theme of the heart because the Psalms are so redolent of that theme. We can link the heart (as we do in our everyday speech) to our deepest desires. If our desires are good and pure—those desires that are the deepest within us—we are living the life of the Beatitudes.

Charles Taylor says (in his recent overwritten book on the roots of secularity) that the rise of devotion to the Sacred Heart was parallel to the emotive spiritual life of the Pietists and the Wesleyans of the same period. It is not about that kind of thinking regarding the concept of heart that I want to pursue, although thinking about the heart of Jesus as a once vibrant spiritual exercise is a rich thing to do. At his deepest level was a heart directed to the Father. It is easy to forget that our own basilica here on campus is under the name "Sacred Heart."

———————————■———————————

In a popular little book on holiness, Jesuit William O'Malley heads his chapters with titles that one would not first think of for such a book (e.g., trust, honesty, impartiality, gratitude, awareness, empathy, perseverance, etc.), but what he unfolds is in fact a classical approach to holiness. Good teacher that he is, he knows that to offer the ideal of holiness to young people, one had better not start with a "churchy" vocabulary. He knows that grace builds on nature and hence his approach. He is not far from a fine tradition in contemporary spirituality, to wit, that to be a holy person is to be a whole person. The one danger of this approach, of course, is to allow Christian spirituality ending up like some form of pop psychology. I want to show this little book to the students in the class for deacons this coming week as we work through our understanding of holiness in the course on spiritual theology.

———————————■———————————

Our world is not in Christ, Thomas Merton said somewhere (I am paraphrasing), but in thrall to images and pictures of Christ. I thought about that very fine insight yesterday while watching some television preacher. Normally, I never linger with those people but this guy was so unctuous, so off-putting, so creepily judgmental that I watched despite myself as if his stupidity and narrowness held me in bonds. Good Lord, no wonder more and more people are disaffiliated from Christianity in this country. If that person was sincere (who can doubt it?) we can only be grateful that his power is limited to preaching on television. One of the biggest problems facing Christianity today is not that we can't reach people; the problem is that these preachers reach too many people for a moment and, because of that moment, most people say *that* is Christianity and, in the next breath, add: ridiculous.

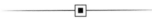

Recently it was reported that one out of every hundred men in this country is in prison. That is an appalling statistic! We are a very punitive society. Just recently there was a flurry of angry letters to the newspaper because a cop-killer "only" got sixty-five years in prison. Sixty-five years! It has been debated in Europe whether or not life in prison without a possibility of parole is inhumane. We, in this country, are still fighting to execute people. Why are we so vindictive? Certain people need to be restrained from life in civil society, but surely we can be more imaginative than to incarcerate so many for such a long time. It is not merely a matter of economics; this is a moral issue that somebody who knows what he is talking about ought to write about in a sensible fashion.

P.S. I need to think about the word "prisoner" and how it is used in the New Testament.

The Samaritan woman says to Jesus, "Give to me this water that I may not thirst again" (Jn 4:15). Of course, in a typical moment of Johannine misunderstanding she is asking for the wrong thing. Nonetheless, this is one of those requests, properly understood, that makes a wonderful prayer; it is also a profoundly moving moment conjuring up all those moments in the biblical tradition where water and the thirst for water plays out in profound ways. The whole scene is reminiscent of all those Old Testament moments when things take place around a well. It struck me—and this for the first time—that there is a paradox here: Jesus promises living water that will satiate all thirst but, on the cross, Jesus himself cries out "I thirst." It is that yearning for water that is so poignant in the Bible; it has its metaphorical moment in the Psalms: "As the deer yearn for living water . . ."

When one stops and reflects back on these kinds of things it is easy to understand how the old fathers of the church could wring so much out of a text.

Still working through John 4. I like that flat statement (verse 23), "the hour is coming and it is now"—it is the tension between "coming" and "is now" that strikes me so forcefully. John loves to fiddle around with the concept of the "hour"

as not coming yet (e.g., the marriage feast of Cana), and the "hour" that becomes fulfilled on the cusp of the crucifixion that gives such a dialectical quality to John's discourse.

<hr/>

This year (2008) Saint Patrick's Day will fall during Holy Week. Hence, a flurry of calls from the media about what the local bishops will do—these feast days of saints are not typically "moveable feasts." Despite the Irish blood coursing through my veins, I have never been that big a fan of those festivities— all those drunks marching down the streets gussied up with the wearing of the Green. Dyeing the river that runs through Chicago emerald green always merits a picture in somebody's newspaper. Of course, it is those who depend on cash flow who are most worried: bar owners, purveyors of corned beef and cabbage; Chinese wage slaves making the junk worn on the day and so on. Bah! Humbug! It is probably my Lithuanian blood (the maternal side of the family) that makes me grumpy or, at least, somewhat indifferent about these matters. That is not to say, however, that I am indifferent about Patrick himself. In fact, some years ago I wrote an introductory essay for a volume of his famous *Confessions*—that little assignment led me to read a lot of Patrician scholarship, which I did willingly.

———■———

Something to explore: Teresa of Avila in chapter 28 of her autobiography says that she had a perception of the humanity of Christ in his risen glory "as it is in pictures." What precisely is the relationship of art to "visions"—what is the nexus between aesthetics and visionary experience? I always ask myself that question when I read the vision of the crucified one described in the early pages of Julian of Norwich. Did she have a heightened grasp of the crucifix carried by the acolyte when the priest came to give her the last rites? What did Francis "see" on Mount La Verna? I always note these descriptions when reading the primary sources, but have never sat down and thought through what these observations, noted especially by autobiographical writers, actually mean.

———■———

At Mass this weekend the responsorial psalm after the first reading: "My soul waits for the Lord/more than those who watch for the morning" (Psalm 130). I felt the awesome strength of those words as the cantor intoned them. I can never think of those few lines from the Psalms without picturing in my mind rows of Trappist monks at Vigils in their white cowls at 3:30 a.m. Monks, true eschatological watchers, are the very incarnation of those lines. Watching. Looking.

Waiting. Such words are powerful instincts on the part of the Christian "not yet."

Good Friday. Of all the holy days of the year, Good Friday seems to me to be the one where ordinary routines seem most out of place. It seems somehow wrong to see stores open as they do a bustling business before the Easter weekend.

Since we do not have class, I usually stay at home listening to the classical radio station which, more often than not, will play a Bach Passion (today it was according to John).

I usually toddle over to the basilica on campus right after lunch in order to find a spot for the ridiculously but edifyingly overcrowded services at 3:00 p.m. A few years ago, I spent the time reading the Lamentations, so this year I backed up and read the opening chapters of Jeremiah. They are wonderful chapters—full of the covenant, the warnings against infidelity, verses that will find their repetition in some of the gospels, some nice lines about the symbolic "watchman" (a theme I love in the Bible) and so on. The couple of hours I spent with Jeremiah was not exactly *lectio divina*—I read too fast—but I read slowly enough to make some head notes in pencil to remind myself to copy out some texts in my notebook.

Read—but at a rapid clip—Cardinal Dziwisz's affectionate memoir of his years as secretary to John Paul II. I learned very little new about the pope that was not more fully reported in George Weigel's biography, although Weigel will be miffed to learn how adamant the pope was in his opposition to the Iraq war (Weigel was dispatched to Rome at the war's offset by the Neocons to instruct the Vatican about the rightness of Bush's war) and how sensitive he was to capitalism's defects. All in all, both this memoir and Weigel's biography, for that matter, had more than a whiff of the hagiographical.

On the Iraq incursion: an act of unmitigated stupidity for which we pay dearly. I write this after a report on the news this morning that the US death toll is 4,000. What a horrendous waste of young life!

For some time I have sought an opportunity to slip in a word like "rodomontade" into print but have been afraid that I would be charged with showing off. It is a shame that such words get unused. Maybe having been once chided by a *Commonweal* editor for calling the argument of a book "risible" has made me gun-shy. I also had an editor for another book strike the word "littoral" and replace it with "shoreline," which was not an improvement in my estimation.

A freshman asked me this morning (in these words), "So, was Jesus a Jew or what?" I kept a straight face and allowed that Jesus was, in fact, a Jew. After the student left, I kept thinking about what was behind the words "or what?"—I could not inquire further since the student had left.

A Few Random Notes on Saints

Saint Margaret Clitherow (pressed to death for her failure to plead) said this of her wealthy husband: "He hath too much; he cannot lift up his head to God for weight of his goods." This is as good a gloss on the problem of the wealthy gaining heaven in Jesus' striking image of the camel passing through the eye of the needle as I have read. It is not the wealth but the gluttony for the wealth that is the issue.

Saint Ivo (Yves) was a Breton lawyer who was not a robber—hence he was a figure of astonishment to his fellow citizens.

Saint Philip Neri: "If you want to be obeyed, don't make commandments."

Winston Churchill on John Foster Dulles: a bull who carries his own china shop with him.

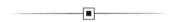

Denys Turner (in *The Darkness of God*) cites this beautiful passage from the thirteenth-century Augustinian Giles of Rome in the latter's commentary on the Song of Songs: "Therefore, the person who studies in order to know, not to build up and make progress in the love of God, should recognize that he leads the contemplative life as the philosophers describe it, not as the theologians do ... the contemplation of the philosophers gives delight to hearing and sight whereas the spiritual contemplation of the theologians gives delight to taste, smell, and touch."

Isaiah 25:6-8 is as good a statement of prophetic universalism as one would hope to find in the Bible. It was cited recently, in a faculty discussion, as a "proof text" for the universal hope of salvation. I do not know if it works or not (what is the status of proof texts such as these?), but it is interesting to take notice that the "feast of rich food" and the "wiping away of tears" is promised to all peoples. When looking the text up to

think about it I read the opening verses of the chapter (verses 1-5), which have the power of a psalm and the beauty of a prayer even though the verses have a certain militant violence about them on the one hand and the promise of refuge for the poor and the needy on the other. Richly rhetorical stuff!

If there is any good example of the tendency of the tradition to embroider, it is to be found in the hagiographical tradition. The early *acta* of the martyrs tend to be quite severe and matter-of-fact: the person is asked by the Roman authorities if he or she is a Christian. An affirmative answer, when asked the third time, brings a swift judgment of condemnation. The *passio*, by contrast, tends to add Christological allusions, longer speeches, diatribes from the inquisitors, and so on. The *legenda* amplifies more with extravagant punishments, miraculous interventions, etc. These embroideries derive from the impulse of the homilist, to be sure, but also, I think, because everybody loves a good story! The legends of the saints are, in effect, pop fiction, even when there might be an historical core somewhere under the imaginative elaborations.

Reading a study of Dietrich Bonhoeffer's theology I was struck by how often he constructs a line that has the ring of the aphorism about it. Some examples:

"God is in the midst of our life beyond it."
"No one possesses God in such a way
that there is no need to await him."
"I am waiting for God." (written on a
scrap while in prison)
"The Church is the place of unshakeable
hope."
"Church is only church when it is there
for others."
"The Church is Christ hidden among us."
"Discipleship is a bond with the
suffering Christ."
"The Man of duty will end up doing his
duty to the Devil as well."
"The religion of Jesus Christ is not the
dessert that comes after the meal but is
rather the bread itself, nothing else."

Bonhoeffer, I read, loved the writings of Georges Bernanos (a passion he shared with Von Balthasar) and, when working on his second doctorate, had read some Edith Stein when she was still a disciple of Husserl. It is so odd to note these crossings among European intellectuals before the War.

Apropos of Bernanos: Harvard psychiatrist Robert Coles once told me that he read *The Diary of a Country Priest* every year. Not a bad practice; it is a wonderful book that was almost successfully put on the screen by Robert Bresson years ago.

A good text for those who are passionate for social justice:

"Open your heart for those who cannot speak" (Proverbs 31:8).

Here is the klutzy version from the NAB: "Open your mouth in behalf of the dumb/and for the rights of the destitute."

Until a student mentioned it in an oral report yesterday in class, I had never known that the phrase "in Christ" occurs over 164 times in the Pauline corpus. Not infrequently, it is read in contrast to something like "in sin" or "in the flesh." The burden of his report was to puzzle out what exactly that phrase meant. I should look up the cognate "in the Spirit" for its frequency. At any event, it is a phrase to which I need to pay more attention when reading Paul. It was not the phrase but the frequency that caught my attention. This is all very important to me because when lecturing on "spirituality" I always use, as my launching point, the critical locus in Romans 8 where Paul contrasts living "in the Spirit" as opposed to living "in the flesh." Utilizing the phrase "in Christ" may flesh out that contrast in Paul.

Later Addendum: In one of his catecheses on Paul, Pope Benedict points out that every now and again, Paul will reverse the "in Christ" to say Christ "in you" (e.g., Rom 8:10; 2 Cor 13:5).

In reading some of these catecheses given by Benedict XVI on the lives of apostles, I have been struck about how the pope can subsume the work of exegetes to his larger purpose; he will note in passing that certain problems (e.g., the authorship of the various works assigned to John) can "best be left to the exegetes." I admire both the craftsmanship of his talks and their theological depth. He both speaks and writes with a studied elegance but always for the larger end of teaching. One of the most significant things about his ministry as pope has been his resistance to "out-performing" his predecessor. Someone recently remarked in print that Ratzinger did not like the cult of personality that grew up around John Paul. There is good reason for that. John Paul so centered himself that the bishops (in some cases, deservedly so) became spear carriers in his opera. Benedict, I think, would resist that kind of adulation. He makes it his business to see himself, rightly, as the center of episcopal unity, not above it.

I do not much keep up with baseball but do enjoy going to games here on campus once the weather warms up. Here are the things I like most: the slow nature of the game (one can actually read between innings, and I am not the only one who does it); the "townie" crowd who come to games—older guys who follow the sport religiously and almost liturgically critique the umpires; the knowledge that winter is over (in football season, the days get cooler; in baseball, warmer); the stylized motion of players, which is like watching great dance; and remembering my father, who loved to go to games in Florida to root for the Cardinals—his favorite team.

I ran across this simplified version of Saint Teresa of Avila's famous prayer (in a book on the Compostella pilgrimage), which is used as one of those Taize chants:

Nada te turbe
Nada te espante
Todo se pasa
Solo Dios no se muda.

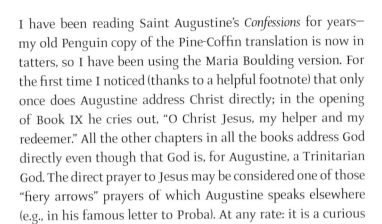

I have been reading Saint Augustine's *Confessions* for years—
my old Penguin copy of the Pine-Coffin translation is now in
tatters, so I have been using the Maria Boulding version. For
the first time I noticed (thanks to a helpful footnote) that only
once does Augustine address Christ directly; in the opening
of Book IX he cries out, "O Christ Jesus, my helper and my
redeemer." All the other chapters in all the books address God
directly even though that God is, for Augustine, a Trinitarian
God. The direct prayer to Jesus may be considered one of those
"fiery arrows" prayers of which Augustine speaks elsewhere
(e.g., in his famous letter to Proba). At any rate: it is a curious
and striking fact about his *Confessions*.

In some Episcopalian publication I ran across a "Stations"
for the week after Easter—known in the Eastern tradition as
"Bright Week." Done as a parallel to the traditional fourteen
stations they run:

> Jesus rises from the dead.
> Women encounter an angel at the tomb.
> Peter and John visit the tomb with Mary
> of Magdala.
> Jesus appears to Mary Magdalene.

Mary Magdalene proclaims the
Resurrection to the apostles.
Jesus appears on the road to Emmaus.
Jesus gives the apostles the power to
forgive.
Jesus confirms the faith of Thomas.
Jesus eats with his disciples on Tiberius
shore.
Jesus forgives Peter and commissions
him.
Jesus gives the great commission to the
disciples.
Jesus ascends to heaven.
Mary and the disciples keep vigil for the
Spirit's advent.
Jesus sends the Holy Spirit.

There are any number of scriptural texts that Saint Augustine
goes back to time and again (think of the line "the letter kills
but the spirit gives life," which so touched him in his attempt,
as he reports it in the *Confessions*, to understand scripture
correctly) but if I were to choose a "touchstone" text (in the
Arnoldian sense of the term) in Augustine I think it would
be that fragment from Galatians 5:6: "faith working through
love." It is at the core of his understanding of faith—as the

Enchiridion makes clear; it is also at the heart of Benedict's approach to faith in his homilies and discourses—no surprise there given the pope's predilection for Augustine.

For the nearly two decades that I have been at Notre Dame there have been discussions about the nature of Catholic education in general and the university in particular; I have been a part of many of these discussions. Recently, looking at Eliot's famous "Notes Towards the Definition of Culture," I was struck by his observation that education has two ends: the formation of character and the transmission of culture. It strikes me that it is possible to "tweak" those two points as a starting point when thinking about the Catholic university. Formation of character can be read as the cultivation of faith both individually and socially (since we are not about the education school model of "character education") in a more robust theological manner, just as we can think of the transmission of culture more broadly as providing an education from within the matrix of Catholic intellectual ideals, especially as "grace building upon nature." Eliot's observations are a bit too neutrally construed to satisfy the needs of our particular situation but, given that, they are not irrelevant.

———————————■———————————

In a paper delivered recently (at a Lumen Christi seminar at the University of Chicago), Denys Turner of Yale made a point that is obvious but to which I have not attended sufficiently: the relationship of Eucharist to resurrection. That relationship is encapsulated in those wonderful lines *nobis pignus datur futurae gloriae.*

Turner tied that observation to an equally profound one, namely, that the Eucharist is made up of both presence and absence; here as sacramental reality and only fully present in the beatific union where there will be no Eucharist since it is a *pignus* (a pledge) of what is to come, and in the beatific vision the pledge is redeemed.

———————————■———————————

The letters of Paul are full of short aphorisms like, "Jesus is Lord" or "Christ Jesus" (i.e., the Messiah is Jesus) and so on. Pelikan, in his compendium of creeds and confessions of faith, has gathered lots of them. They constitute what Von Balthasar has penetratingly called *ganze im fragment*—everything in fragment. They are "everything" in the sense that the fragment crystallizes the core faith of Christianity in a very brief couple of words.

Saint Irenaeus's small observation, "The Glory of God is the person fully human" (*Gloria Dei homo vivens*) can be rightly attributed to the Incarnation. It also strikes me that it is also a useful launching pad for a statement of social justice. After all, for a person to be fully human it is necessary that such a person not only has primordial rights to be fed, housed, clothed, and so on but to be in such a position to *flourish*—to have hope, freedom, and space to grow emotionally, socially, spiritually, and intellectually. It is a profound little statement to remember every time we read about those who are oppressed, beaten down, used, neglected, and so on. Again, one sees the deep nexus between the Incarnation and social justice.

In an autobiographical reflection in the philosopher Roger Scruton's book of essays, *Gentle Regrets*, he makes a point worth jotting down. The poignant loss of faith reflected in Arnold's poem "Dover Beach" is one that must be seen in the context of an erosion of the traditional religious verities of Victorian England (Arnold wrote the poem in 1867) whereas, by contrast, and only a generation or so later, Nietzsche's rejection of those same verities must be read against a yawning chasm of nihilism. There is a gentle sadness in Arnold whereas in Nietzsche there is a yelp of triumph, much like that of the contemporary militant atheists who, in Scruton's words, are "welcoming our liberation from the chains of faith." The Arnold/Nietzsche contrast is his better point—and correct, in my judgment, to boot. His conclusion is also interesting: the scientific optimists today join Nietzsche in welcoming the liberation from faith, while the cultural pessimists join Arnold "in his subdued lamentation." One could name names.

One would be hard-pressed to think of a single verse in Augustine that served as a key to understanding him, but one part of a verse surely unlocks his analysis of faith and comes at the tail end of Galatians 5:6, "faith working through love." It is the lens through which almost all of his analysis of faith in the first part of his *Enchiridion* (which I am currently reading) operates. That intimate connection between faith and love is all over Benedict's encyclicals, especially his *Deus Caritas Est*. Worth noting: the verse begins, "the only thing that counts is faith working through love."

A nice *mot*: "He is as nervous as a Christian Scientist with appendicitis."

———————◼———————

I heard a homily a few days ago at which the preacher "ex-plained" a doctrine that sounded like he took it right out of some elementary theology textbook (or from *Wikipedia*?). It was accurate, but it was a handful of dust. Here is what Walter Brueggemann says in his book on the prophetic imagination: "The Church must be a poetic community." Such a commu-nity offers explosive, concrete, critical images in order to help people "reorganize their lives." That is why, I think, Jesus told stories and scattered images all over the place: look at the lily; consider the mustard seed; and so on. Of course, the danger is that the preacher might be tempted (often is tempted) to drag out some banal image from the latest offerings on the television screen. Being a poetic church is, especially for the preacher (and the teacher as well!), tough if we lack the touch for poetry.

———————◼———————

Giving a series of conferences recently to a community of reli-gious sisters on the tradition of mystical prayer, it struck me that my exposition was a bit too academic; but it began to get a good reception when I insisted that many of the sisters probably had "mystical" experiences but did not have the vo-cabulary to describe them. Some seemed to have the idea that their moments when they were silent and intensely conscious of the presence of God in their life were not "mystical" because they did not have any of the epiphenomena often associated with mystical prayer. John of the Cross, however, was not keen on such experiences (he is alleged to have said that he would not walk across a plaza to visit a stigmatic!). I also noted that Jean Gerson in his treatise on the subject had a whole range of nouns to describe mystical prayer, which he rightly described as the "experiential knowledge of God that comes from the embrace of unitive love." Nicely put! I underscored at length the adjective "experiential"—an experience that is not simply cognitive—I also linked his adjective with the classic statement *amor ipse notitia est*—that is, love is a kind of knowledge.

Of course, I did all this while making no claims about being a mystic!

Barth said in so many words that "to clasp the hands in prayer is the beginning of the uprising against the disorders of the world." I am especially taken with the noun "uprisings," since one rarely sees that word juxtaposed to prayer. It would seem like so much rhetoric had Barth not been so active in the Confessing Church until the Nazis showed him the door.

In *On True Religion (De Vera Religione)* Augustine makes the nice point that even though some of the pagan philosophers had grasped eloquent truths (which at times some of the fathers like Justin believed they got from the Old Testament prophets), they still paid homage to the pagan pantheon. True Religion is the one in which there is a harmony between cult and belief—that is the basis for authentic *intellectus fidei*—with authentic understanding of the faith. That, after all, is why the Creed is recited in common at the liturgy.

I am reading a new biography of Nietzsche—poor man! All those migraines, stomach upsets, failing eyesight; no wonder he was so splenetic. I am also struck by all the wandering, and the checking in and out of hotels, spas, and so many unheated trains seeking some place to rest and write. I can even forgive him for his quondam adulation of the horrible Richard Wagner. Despite all that, he was a titanic writer and thinker. His ending was quite sad and made all the more so because he fell into the clutches of his horrible sister, Elizabeth, who turned him into some kind of grotesque saint to be enshrined in a vulgar mansion she acquired in order to wheel him out as a kind of idol for her adoring friends.

In one of his sermons to the newly baptized (Sermon no. 272), Saint Augustine says that the word "sacramentum" can be described as one thing being seen while another thing is understood. That is an economical but profound observation. He was making this point apropos of the Eucharist: one sees the bread but, in faith, something else is understood.

I ran across that sermon in the collection of Augustine's *Essential Sermons* (New City Press), which I am reading a bit of each day. I should get all eleven volumes of the sermons in the new English version but am too cheap to put out all the required money and too lazy to go over to the library to check them out volume by volume.

Some years ago, the late Saul Bellow gave an interview to *Le Monde*. While speaking about the secularization of France, he said that nobody in France believes in God, and thus God ends up sitting in a café all day long. God, in France, is not hidden; God is emeritus.

The notion of an emeritus God carries with it a small insight; there may be a lingering sense of God in secular affairs, but it is as if God has retired from the ongoing life of such societies. *Mutatis mutandis*, the same thing may be said of the god of common political discourse in this country. It is a far cry from Pascal's God of Abraham, Isaac, and Jacob; it is the god of the philosophers.

In readying myself to write a short essay on the sin of "sloth," I was struck by the fact that in the ancient church sloth was equated with sadness (*tristitia*), melancholy, and proximity to despair, whereas in our contemporary world it is a synonym for laziness or lack of energy. Sloth translates *acedia* and must not be rendered down to an adjective describing someone lounging about in bed until lunchtime. The early monks saw it as a terrible temptation, equating it with the famous "noon day devil" of Psalm 91:6—a psalm (Psalm 90 in the Vulgate) which is sung in monasteries every night at Compline as Saint Benedict legislates in his *Rule.* Many early monks saw *acedia* as a temptation worse than pride because it could lead to despair.

Prudentius, the Spanish-born Christian poet of the late fourth century, composed some inscriptions (*tituli*) that were used under mosaics or frescos in some Christian churches. There are over forty of them written in rather elegant Latin. I was struck by something I had never known before: in the one on the returning dove to Noah's ark, Prudentius explains that the raven did not come back because it could land on the corpses of the drowned, but the dove would never do that. Evidently, this explanation was not uncommon among the fathers to solve a question: what happened to the raven Noah first sent out?

I found out this curious fact while looking up something else in Prudentius.

Speaking of nice biblical observations (see above entry!), Augustine makes the very apt point (in a sermon on almsgiving) that Zacchaeus the Publican climbed up a tree to get a look at the One who would later hang from a tree. I love those kinds of readings when one runs across them in the fathers.

I have always assumed that the three theological virtues of faith, hope, and charity all derive from the end of the great hymn on charity in 1 Corinthians 13, but recently I see that Paul uses that triad with some frequency. Faith, hope, and charity are embedded by name in Romans 5:15 and, in a somewhat different order, in Colossians 1:4-5. Just recently, I came across a third usage in 1 Thessalonians 1:3: "Remembering before our God and Father your work of faith and labor of love and steadfastness of hope in our Lord Jesus Christ." During this year of Saint Paul (2008-2009), it would be good to go back over those texts and see how they fit the broader context of Paul's thinking—there is a good meditation to be found there.

A young man came by my office the other day to inquire about graduate studies. He became a Catholic while in the hospital being treated for a form of brain cancer. Someone gave him Thomas Merton's *Thoughts in Solitude*, which was the first step towards his conversion. Every time I hear a story like that I would like to share it with those *bien pensants* who refused to include Merton's biography in the catechism for young adults. Our bishops are so timid! I hear stories like this all the time. Just this morning I got an inquiry from a rabbi who is writing a thesis on Abraham Heschel, who has been reading Merton. Ah well, the prophet is without honor in his own country.

My colleague Ann Astell gave me, as a birthday gift, the new Marquette University edition of Dorothy Day's journals and diaries. In a small act of asceticism, I read only ten pages or so a day. In the diaries of the late 1950s and into the 1960s I have a feeling of *déjà vu* as I read what she was reading—books of my youth: Alban Goodier, van Zeller, et al.

Speaking of Dorothy Day: Colman McCarthy in his book *I'd Rather Teach Peace* (which every teacher ought to read!) notes that while there is a big effort to canonize Day, it is worthwhile noting that when she died, not one bishop came to her funeral! The late Cardinal Cooke asked that the funeral's time be changed, but the Workers said no because doing so would interfere with the morning bread line.

Rabbi Michael Signer, who joined our faculty the same year I did (1988), has pancreatic cancer. He mentioned in an e-mail that he is sustained each day by reading Psalm 23. As a consequence, we have all decided as a department to say the same psalm each day in solidarity with him. I told him a few weeks ago that as an atavistic Catholic, I was going to light a candle at the Grotto on campus. A few days later, after having a rough chemo treatment in Chicago, he sent me a message: did I light the candle yet?

Sitting next to an old alumnus at a football game (which we were winning) he turned to me spontaneously and said with feeling, "I have never been happier in my life!" I have had the same tickets for nearly twenty years surrounded by old timers who, not even meaning to, are hilarious. Somehow I enjoy those hours with the crowd almost as much as I enjoy the games given my own limited appetite for organized sports.

Augustine loved to quote a line from Isaiah: "Unless you believe you will not understand" (7:9). Alas, that line (which Augustine knew in the Old Latin) comes from the Septuagint and is not found in our bibles; it was almost a talisman for Augustine (as it was for others) so here is a mildly curious fact: he was inspired by a biblical tag which may not have been biblical at all.

At Sunday Mass in Antigua (Guatemala) the priest recited the Creed as a series of questions as they do at the time of baptism. To each of the three great Trinitarian questions the congregation responded. While that was happening, I was forcefully reminded of the young Thomas Merton in Cuba where he had an overwhelming spiritual experience as children thundered out "Yo creo!" (I believe) in a Franciscan church in Havana. Merton recounts this in his *Secular Journal*. That moment for me in Antigua was simultaneously a powerful moment of memory and a deep sense of communion, not only with Merton but with all who respond in the same manner. I thought about that moment all day as I trudged through the cobblestone streets of Antigua.

Peter Kropotkin in *Mutual Aid*: think about what kind of world you want to live in—ask what you need to know to create that world—demand that your teachers teach you that.

Charles Taylor's book *A Secular Age* has a powerful concluding chapter on conversion—as good as anything I have read. I am using ideas from it for some stuff I am writing about prayer.

On the way to work this morning I was mesmerized watching a hawk (red tailed?) trying to get into striking position to pick off a pigeon perched on one of the huge lights over the football stadium, and in so watching, I almost walked into a tree.

I wonder if it is the same hawk who sits alertly up in the lights of the soccer stadium.

I just finished reading the newly published journals of
Dorothy Day. Should she get canonized, it will be the first
time that we have a saint's portrait who was upfront about
her own body. Undramatically, she talks about her sexual
longings even while celibate: her failing body as she got older, with notes about sagging breasts; stomach problems and
toothaches; pains in her legs and feet; and so on. She puts
down those problems matter-of-factly, with no self-pity and
few adornments of pseudo-piety: no "offering up" uncomfort-
able shoes, etc. There are patches where her piety and love of
God shine off the page, as does her intense devotion to the
poor—even those drinkers, madmen, bag ladies, and eccentrics
who were taken into the various Catholic Worker houses. It
was those latter entries that made me think how far away
from Christian heroism I am; the idea of living in a house full
of drunk and mentally unstable people, or eccentrics to the
point of lunacy, would be beyond me.

Even though the worst of the sexual abuse crisis seems to be
behind us, it is to be wondered at how much moral authority
the bishops of this country have lost. They have semi-annual
meetings, and they issue statements that nobody reads; many
people think that they are obsessed about "life" issues such as

abortion. One must ask: are they prophets crying out in the wilderness, or is there another way to confront this problem with less rhetoric and more . . . what? One of the problems is that so many of the bishops, though not all, especially those appointed under John Paul II, are so mediocre intellectually and so insular in their worldview and, worst of all, so timid.

Most weekday mornings I go and swim for half an hour early in the morning. It is for the sake of my health. Swimming is very boring—back and forth until 500 meters or so is done. It is a quiet contemplative form of exercise made burdensome only when the lifeguard insists on blasting a local radio program of rock-and-roll over the loud speaker in the fear that things are too quiet in the pool. It is on the way to my car from the pool that I feel good, not so much because I am invigorated by the exercise, but because I feel so damned virtuous for doing it.

A lot of people around my age and younger seem to be dying; within a week Richard John Neuhaus (whom I knew slightly) and my close friend and colleague Michael Signer both died of cancer. Michael and I were good friends; he an ordained rabbi with a keen interest in Christianity, and I a Christian with a fascination with Judaism and always ashamed that my Hebrew was almost non-existent. It was to Michael that I went to get leads on whom to read and what to study; he would come to me to parse the most recent statements from the Vatican (often I counseled benign skepticism). Some weeks before his death I spent an afternoon with him, which we spent as we often did: telling jokes, engaging in non-malicious gossip, and talking shop. I miss him badly and do not even like to walk by his now-silent office a floor below me. Michael was a mensch in the full Yiddish meaning of the word.

At Christmas morning Mass in the Lower East Side, a street person complete with a roll-on basket (pinched perhaps from a local supermarket?) to carry his collected newspapers and other stuff came into church just a little bit late. He knew the drill (genuflecting, kneeling, sitting, and so on). He changed pews three or four times and chatted up those seated there. After Mass my daughter said that she was frightened that he would come to our pew. I told her that I was kind of glad to see him; it would be a sad day when anyone would eject an old, addled street person from Mass; it was a nice Christmas moment. As we were leaving, he said that his parents were dead and he wanted to know if we would adopt him, but we declined. I am sure he ate at the Catholic Worker-sponsored Saint Joseph's House, which was nearby, and as we returned to my daughter's apartment I thought of Dorothy Day, who spent decades with such folks on these very streets; streets increasingly gentrified.

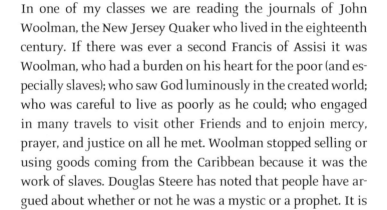

In one of my classes we are reading the journals of John Woolman, the New Jersey Quaker who lived in the eighteenth century. If there was ever a second Francis of Assisi it was Woolman, who had a burden on his heart for the poor (and especially slaves); who saw God luminously in the created world; who was careful to live as poorly as he could; who engaged in many travels to visit other Friends and to enjoin mercy, prayer, and justice on all he met. Woolman stopped selling or using goods coming from the Caribbean because it was the work of slaves. Douglas Steere has noted that people have argued about whether or not he was a mystic or a prophet. It is clear to me that his (very gentle) prophetic message grew out of a profound sense of the hidden presence (and for him, at times, not so hidden) sense of the presence of God.

While reading Woolman I discovered that a Notre Dame professor, now at the University of Rochester, has just written a very fine book on Woolman rightly entitled *The Beautiful Soul of John Woolman* (Hill and Wang)—by Thomas Slaughter.

While eating in restaurants in New York I noticed that people were constantly checking their Blackberries for messages and/or texting someone. My older daughter does it constantly. Is this a new form of addiction? Yesterday, my computer froze up for a few hours and I found myself anxious because it was impossible to send or receive e-mails. Those untethered two hours had me vaguely unsettled—something is wrong about this.

Among the writings of Thomas More is one entitled *De Tristitia Christi*—On the Sadness of Christ. There is a lot one could say about that topic.

Yesterday I looked out a window into our backyard to see that a hawk (or maybe a peregrine falcon; it was hard to tell) had nailed a squirrel under the bird feeder and was busy tearing it apart and eating it. There were patches of vividly scarlet blood spatters on the snow. The poet Tennyson was right: nature red in tooth and claw. It was an awesomely beautiful (is that the right word?) sight. I watched for a bit until the meal was over. Evidently, the raptor took what was left with it, for there was only the bloodstain to mark the event.

While reading Matthias Scheeben's *The Mysteries of Christianity*—still powerful more than a century after it first appeared—I learned that in the early tradition the Holy Spirit was sometimes called the *jubilus Patris et Filii*. For a long time I kept wondering how to translate that word *jubilus* so as to catch the clamorous joy behind the word; I could not come up with an English equivalent. Would "exhilaration" serve?

At Mass this past Saturday evening the lector read (from Saint Paul) that our bodies were not made for immortality, instead of saying "immorality." Neither the celebrant nor the congregation noticed the mistake although I did (with a bit of amusement) because I had been teaching that epistle the previous week in class.

With monotonous regularity my phone begins to ring in early February (it happened this morning) to ask about Saint Valentine. I have a well-rehearsed answer about how the feast day of the saint (February 14) commemorates a martyr by that name (perhaps two martyrs—one in Rome; the other from Narni—the sources are unclear), how it became associated with the coming of Spring (Chaucer mentions the day when birds chose their mates) and, little by little, became associated with proposals for marriage. Enter Hallmark, rose growers, chocolate peddlers, etc., and there you have it. And the sainted martyr(s)? They got bumped off the calendar by Saints Cyril and Methodius.

Rummaging around in my cluttered desk drawer I ran across a photograph of Michael Signer and myself standing near the *cardo* in the Old City of Jerusalem, dated 1997. I was quite slim and he vibrantly youthful. Less than a month ago, he, ravaged by pancreatic cancer, died. I felt both old and bereft looking at that photo. I remember later that same day we walked to the Western Wall.

Was it on that same trip that, on another day, I was on the Temple Mount when Jon Sobrino felt faint (he is a diabetic) and left us to find a cab to take him back to Tantur?

A student told me how, when he runs in the evening, he prays as he makes his way around the lakes on campus. When students tell me such things I wonder if I am worthy to claim to be their teacher.

How often we see the wonderful phrase "the face of God" in the Bible. Saint Anselm, in the opening of the *Proslogion* uses the image of the "Face of God" (from the Psalms) as a prayerful refrain as he seeks to understand God.

When the midwives failed to report the birth of Hebrew children (in Exodus), were they the first examples of civil disobedience?

In reading Saint Thomas recently I ran across his observation explaining why the Eucharist involves both bread and wine. Thomas advances three reasons: first, to symbolize the passion; second, that it is food and drink; and third, for the health of body and soul (*anima*). Was Thomas saying that bread is for the body and wine for the health of the soul? Curious.

Terry Tilley argues (in *The Disciples' Jesus*) that the gospels are the end product of the active imagination of the first disciples. That is an excellent point but one must explain what he is driving at so that a naïve person does not mistake "active imagination" for "imaginary," as in "made up." His point is that the gospels are a way of saying: here is how the memory of Jesus impacted me and, by extension, my community.

In the *De Doctrina Christiana* Augustine says—almost in passing —that we followers of the Way have as our pavement Christ himself, who undergirds our path. It is an odd but fruitful image and the first time I have ever come across it. Augustine, of course, has a finely tuned set of antennas for detecting Christological motifs in the scriptures.

I recently received a book that has some sayings from the old desert fathers and mothers so arranged that there is a reading for each day. The book sits on my desk and I read each day a little, more or less faithfully. Some of those old wisdom sayings are quite wonderful. Here is a small one attributed to

Abba Poemen: "At the moment when a person goes astray, if he says 'I have sinned' immediately the sin ceases."

Rereading Bonhoeffer's *The Cost of Discipleship* (with my class in spiritual writers), which is, in my estimation, one of the great classics of spiritual writing in the twentieth century. The work is profoundly biblical and profoundly sophisticated. It takes on a greater luminosity when one realizes that it was written in the late 1930s in the dark days of German National Socialism. In less than a decade after its publication Bonhoeffer will be hanged by the Gestapo on direct orders from Himmler.

Lent—the word derives from the Middle English *lente,* which means "springtime," although frequently the beginning of Lent is only giving us a distant hope for spring!

The flap *du jour*: Pope Benedict, in attempting to reconcile four dissident bishops of the Society of Saint Pius X, did not seem to know that one of these bishops is a notorious Holocaust Denier. Apart from the fact that the Vatican fact-checkers were asleep at the wheel, it is also the case, not sufficiently realized, that *a priori*, the society itself attracts a lot of fanatics who loathe modern freedom and reconciliation with the Jews and detect Masons behind every bush, tree, and every opening made manifest at Vatican II. They are a textbook example of what happens when you mix religious rigidity with extreme nationalism. The late Marcel LeFebvre, their founder, was a friend of the Vichy Government, an admirer of Franco in Spain, Pinochet in Chile, and Salazar in Portugal. The Society of Saint Pius X is to Catholicism what those rabbinical fundamentalists who hole up in Hebron are to Judaism or those Islamic mullahs who issue *fatwas* indiscriminately or the ultra nationalist Hindus who wreak such havoc in India today. A pox on all of them!

Taking to heart the advice of those wise spiritual guides who say that we should do something rather than give up something for Lent, I read, last year, the Isaiah volume in the "Church's Bible" series—the text, plus patristic and early medieval commentary. This year I have tucked into my bag a volume in the same series on 1 Corinthians. Some years ago I intended to read all four gospels in Greek—managed to stay with the Greek but only got through Mark. There is something to be said for reading the Bible in a different language because it forces one to slow down. Because we think we "know" the English text, we tend to skim over the gospels too rapidly. One suggestion Michael Casey, the Australian Trappist, made was to read the text out loud—that does slow down the process. He also does not approve of marking up the text with underlining or side notes. In this I cannot follow him as my much-annotated bibles will attest. I have a penchant for such jotting—my copy of Augustine's *Confessions* is like a rainbow, since I use a different colored pen every time I read it. In fact, I have had to lay aside my Penguin copy since the pages are now falling out, so I have begun to mark up my Boulding translation.

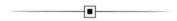

I like the Latin word *mansuetudo* because its English equivalent—meekness—sounds so namby-pamby (meek as lambs and all that). Saint Thomas says that it is the virtue whose opposite is anger. Do we have a better word than "meekness"?

Today a student, while discussing Gregory of Nyssa's *Life of Moses*, asked, "Does everything in the Bible have a deeper meaning?" "Yes," I replied.

Today someone wrote me to tell me that an old friend (we go back forty years) has Parkinson's disease and the early stages of dementia. One of the ominous things about getting old is not only one's own infirmities but the frequent news of the worse infirmities of others when one imagines them to be forever young. It explains why, among other reasons, I resist going to reunions—too much clearly evident decrepitude.

The other evening, public television ran the BBC version of *Oliver Twist*. Among his many other gifts, Dickens had a gift for making up fictional names. Could a would-be beadle of the poor house be anyone else than Mister Bumble? "Bumble the Beadle" just has a certain ring to it that is exactly right.

For a couple of courses I have used Michael Casey's valuable book on prayer (*Toward God*). I like to point out to students a couple of his "throwaway" lines that can be, but should not be, overlooked:

> There is no evidence at all in the
> Christian tradition that sin disqualifies
> us from prayer. (p. 156)

Nothing in the life can put us outside
the range of God's mercy. (p. 157)

Here is the redoing of Anselm's famous definition of theology as "faith seeking understanding" from the late Dominican friar, Herbert McCabe: "thinking about what God has told us." The ever-witty McCabe said, towards the end of his life, that humans live through three stages: youth, maturity, and "You're looking good today."

Psalm 99 has a triple invocation of the holiness of God that I have never noticed before—the thrice-repeated "Holy is God" occurs in verses 3 and 5 with the added emphatic "Holy is the Lord, our God" in verse 9. It makes a nice parallel to the more famous cry in the temple from the prophet Isaiah, which we recite at the end of the preface to the Eucharistic prayer in the liturgy.

I am doing some reading in preparation for one of my final essays (for *Notre Dame Business*) on the seven deadly sins. The subject is "lust," so I can walk about claiming I am doing research on lust (or maybe I won't say it—to be on the safe side and not scandalize the brethren).

We are reading Simone Weil in class—she is one of those tortured souls (like Pascal and SK) who are to be wondered at but not emulated. I always feel a bit sad when I read her work, but there is something quite compelling about her.

I have been working on a commencement address for Saint Anselm's College. These are very difficult speeches to write because one's mind is first flooded with banalities, truisms, and high-flown sentiments. I think I am going to focus on two words from Anselm's famous definition of theology, since this speech will occur during the 900th anniversary of his death. The words are "seeking," since life is a search, and "understanding" (*intellectum*), because true understanding is closer to King Solomon's prayer for an "understanding heart" than it is to knowledge (*scientia*). I will have to muse over these words a bit before putting pen to paper.

Should I start with a witticism? My favorite line for such occasions is one made by the "Doonesbury" author (Gary Trudeau), who said that commencement speeches sedate students before launching them into the larger world.

I am thrilled to be invited to the college for two reasons: I am partial to monks and their founding community is Benedictine and, secondly, I love the writings of Saint Anselm because his most original work (e.g., the *Proslogion*) is set within the context of a prayerful reading of scripture.

Going to the college will be a great treat since I have never before been in the state of New Hampshire.

Sergius Bulgakov's book on Mary (*The Burning Bush*) has a long critique of the Catholic dogmatic teaching on the Immaculate Conception. He believes in the sinlessness of Mary, but thinks that the Catholic notion of a *donum superadditum* is all wrong. B. wrote that book in the 1920s and one cannot wonder but that had he written it much later, after de Lubac's *Surnaturel*, he might have had a different take on matters.

This interest in matters of Mariology has been triggered by a request that I write a long review essay on some recent works on Mary—I dutifully read them and turned in circa 3,000 words, which has led me to do some more thinking about Our Lady. Now, a request comes for me to speak on Mary as part of a Hesburgh lecture series in Tennessee—I will think this over since in the coming year I also have to write a paper on the

spirituality of cathedrals and also prepare seven short meditations on the last words of Jesus for Good Friday—the former
talk is for Milwaukee and the latter for Spokane. Currently, I
am working on a paper for the upcoming Newman Conference
to be held here in just a few months—the topic is prayer in the
Parochial and Plain Sermons. Most of that lecture is written, but
my best line is not on prayer but an aside to the effect that
those sermons are neither plain nor parochial.

There is vast profundity in a line Karl Rahner wrote in 1937 apropos of prayer: "You have seized me; I have not grasped You."
That is Rahner, very much the mystic, writing those lines.

I ran into another interesting etymological point the other
day while reading about the making of the King James Bible.
Evidently, during times of plague, it was commonly thought
that when a person died or was near death with plague symp-
toms, he or she was struck by the wing of the angel of death.
That angelic touch—a stroke (Latin: *plaga*)—slowly evolved as
a noun to describe anyone who unexpectedly fell into a state
near death—hence: having a *stroke.*

Our campus was awash for days (or, the entrance to the campus) with pro-life protestors—they were, by and large, a raggedy-assed crew—many of them fundamentalist Protestants who had a small fleet of trucks painted with slogans and carrying posters. All I could do was mutter "Oh! If only Flannery O'Connor were still alive!" If the truth be told, she would have looked on them more sympathetically than I did. This is probably intellectual snobbery on my part.

Upset alumni (over the pro-abortion speaker at graduation—the president) had pledged not to contribute to Notre Dame until the current president was fired. They claim to have garnered such withheld pledges to the tune of a couple million dollars. I would have been more impressed had they turned in their season tickets for football games.

It struck me forcefully while reading Safranski's biography of Martin Heidegger that it is possible to be a profound intellectual while, at the same time, a perfectly awful human being. It was not only his long engagement with the Nazis in the 1930s (he did nothing to aid Edmund Husserl, who was Jewish, when Husserl lost his academic post), but that he was a serial adulterer, beginning with his seduction of Hannah Arendt.

Heidegger thoroughly and publicly repudiated his Catholicism but, in his old age, when visiting old churches, he would always cross himself and use holy water, explaining to a person who saw him do it that where "there has been much praying, there the divine is present in a very special way." Heidegger stipulated that he be buried in the churchyard of the parish where he was raised (Meßkirch), and a proper Catholic funeral be celebrated.

The newspaper reported that someone just recently paid over $250,000 for a private parking space in some exclusive part of the city of Boston. As a friend of mine once said: it is not the misery of the poor but the excesses of the rich that has turned him into a radical.

While on a recent stay with the Trappists in Kentucky I could not but help noticing how the community ages. What is most interesting, however, is the seeming serenity with which the community deals with that reality. Many are called, few are chosen, and fewer still remain, one of them quipped. Their four novices are all middle-aged. Of course, the culture wars against the very young from settling into a regular life where "fun" or "adventures" or "experiences" are few—the sheer regularity and humility of the life and not the burden of the vows is what makes the life so ascetic. It is the same kind of attitude behind the observation of one of my students who judged the academic life to be "boring" even though, apart from a few mechanical tasks, I never found this life a bore.

Aging! One of my former colleagues in Florida is dying of cancer while another, recently calling me, is showing the first signs of dementia.

One of the most beautiful words in our theological vocabulary: *icon*. The word is now evacuated of all meaning by being overused for everything and everyone who is sort of well-known or pointing towards classic status; thus, recently, the Lamborghini is an iconic automobile, or *Shane* is the iconic Western. I think I am going to spell the word as *ikon*.

Gospel = "Good News." The Gospel must have a vigor and an air of absolute truth. For me, the Eastern Easter greeting is the best example I know. One says, "Christ is risen!" to which another responds, "Christ is truly risen!" Perfect: brief and absolutely true.

One of my personal failings is the inability to shut off the academic impulse when at liturgy. Singing along with the monks during Office I keep thinking about a just-sung line: "That is beautiful—I must write that down in my journal!" Fleetingly, I thought about bringing my notebook to choir—successfully resisted the idea.

I recently ran across a quite fetching and very Anglican line (British version). An elderly woman gave some advice to a younger friend about getting over life's daily disappointments, saying that in her experience, "a hot bath, a glass of whisky and *The Book of Common Prayer*" solves most problems.

————————■————————

It only struck me quite recently (after all these years!) that titles like "The Gospel According to Saint Luke" or one of the other evangelists has a rather important significance. The "according to . . ." means that the sacred writer has not captured the entire "Good News" (Gospel) but his particular version of it. There is one Gospel. That explains why harmonies of the gospels (even an ancient one like Tatian's *Diatessaron*) rather miss the point and why such harmonies are never quite satisfactory. Luke and Matthew felt quite free to take over almost all of Mark because he had a perspective for which they had a reverence.

————————■————————

On a recent visit to New York City, I went to a Sunday morning Mass at a Catholic church on Park Avenue simply because it was near our hotel. It turned out that I had unwittingly chosen a full-blown Tridentine Mass, complete with priest in a biretta with a pom-pom decorating it, fiddleback chasuble, a covey of altar boys, much moving the missal about, and so on. As Mass began I thought I would experience a wave of nostalgia for the old ways but, truth be told, it seemed like a kind of Kabuki play sort of liturgy at which (my rough count) about sixty people watched somewhat passively, even though they did sing the common parts of the Mass in a tentative fashion.

During the sermon I recognized the priest, who is a convert from Anglicanism and who sometimes appears on the television channel (EWTN) giving talks on hymns. He wears a very high collar and wide sash girding up his cassock like some character out of Trollope. The whole liturgy had the air of the antique to it, even though I do like the art in his church. The one thing that I did seem to realize is that I have no strong urge to go back to this ancient rite.

Over the city of Rio there is, set high on a mountain, an enormous statue of Christ with his arms outstretched over the city. That statue is not infrequently hidden in clouds or fog. For that reason the late Brazilian bishop (and mystic) Helder Camara often said that in his life he always sought to see the "unclouded Christ."

I have just been gently scolded by the person in charge of the *Commonweal* blog site for being delinquent in my contributions; that I have been delinquent is a fact. I have tried very hard to wean myself away from reading the plethora of sites that are out there because there is way too much opinion about church matters and some of it is, to put it gently, less than charitable. The Internet is extremely useful and Google a godsend for checking up odd bits of information, but it is also a curse. The commentary on matters Catholic can be so heartless and, often enough, ignorant and malicious. During the lead-up to the 2009 Notre Dame graduation I was bombarded with e-mails condemning our university's president, forwarding to me the most recent comment of bishop X or archbishop Y (some of those comments were stupid and ignorant, and, worse, vitriolic) and, from the other side, letters urging me to sign this manifesto or withhold that contribution. It all took on an air of unreality in which sensible controversy and/or discussion got drowned out in a welter of talk.

The parallel case is—albeit on a more controlled level—the way a picayune piece of political drama can be talked to death on cable news shows on television. Speed and access of communication is not the same as seeking truth (in charity). Of course, the upside of all this is that in a totalitarian society the truth does get out either via cell phone or Internet. The communication revolution, like all revolutions, brings pain as well as gain.

Ronald Knox, in his book *Enthusiasm*, commenting on Tertullian's joining the Montanists: given Tertullian's precise and brilliant Latin writings, it was as shocking as if Cardinal John Henry Newman had joined the Salvation Army. I learned this while reading a new literary biography of Knox. I read a lot of Knox as a young man but, in the main, his writings now seem very much of a past that cannot be recovered. Of that generation only Chesterton still commands attention in "Catholic" writing, while the others are now read mainly for a jaunt down memory lane.

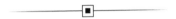

A sign of the times: at a local chain bookstore next to "Religion" there is a section called "Atheism."

The late American painter Paul Cadmus did a series of paintings on the "seven deadly sins" and then added a new one celebrating an eighth deadly sin: "Jealousy." It now hangs in the Metropolitan Museum in New York.

When in New York I tend to revisit some places of which I am particularly fond: the Frick to see Bellini's "The Ecstasy of Saint Francis"; the Strand Bookstore on 14th Street; etc. There is now a new "favorite" place: the "High Line" park near the Hudson River—twenty blocks of what was once a train line now turned into an elevated park with granite pavers, wonderful plantings of flowers, grasses, and shrubs with a liberal scattering of chairs and benches, and *mirabili dictu*, clean convenient rest rooms! One can begin the walk at the end of "Little 12th Street" near where my daughter works and close to one of my favorite eateries (Pastis) on 12th and 9th. It was a great discovery although it might be a bit chilly in the winter if it is open at all (I forgot to ask).

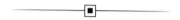

Saint Francis de Sales would ask people: How is your heart?

"The Lord God has given me the tongue of those who are taught that I may know how to sustain with a word him that is weary" (Is 50:4). We should turn that factual statement of Isaiah into a petition.

Balthasar's writings are so copious that it is easy to lose sight of his randomly observed brilliant insights under the sheer welter of his prose. Here, for example, is an illuminating insight in one of his minor works: anyone who sneers at beauty will not be able to pray and if one cannot pray one equally will not be able to love (from *Love Alone*).

I have just finished teaching Julian of Norwich's *Showings* for the umpteenth time. As well as I know the text, it still moves me to read her wonderful vernacular use of English even though we are reading it in contemporary English. I love her use of "courteous" and "homely" and the older uses to which she puts such words as "sport." I once made a whole list of such words in a notebook and have looked in vain for that list but without success.

Thinking of Julian (see note above) reminds me that over the years I had an idea of reading with students the writings of Gertrude of Helfta, but never got around to doing it. It is a shame because, as Cipriano Vagaggini wrote decades ago, if there was a liturgical theologian she was surely one. She lived in the liturgy but also had that beautiful affective piety that one expects to see after the time of Anselm. I have read a fair amount of Gertrude myself and served on a pretty good dissertation committee on her, but never introduced her to my class. Of course, when one surveys the Christian tradition from the Apostolic fathers to the High Middle Ages it is hard to "fit in" everyone. We ought to have a semester on the patristic period, another on the Middle Ages, etc., but, alas, the curriculum does not allow us.

I prefer to read fewer texts and read them thoroughly. A student told me the other day that in a philosophy class they read all of the *Confessions* (all 13 books!) in one week—that is, in my view, a travesty.

I quoted in class this morning a brief tag from Shakespeare ("As flies to wanton boys are we to the gods . . .") and a student said: "King Lear!" And I said (to myself): this intervention has made my day.

Rereading these entries brought to mind a line from Thomas Merton (from his journals?) to the effect that nobody has ever invented a perfect way of wasting time. These various scribbles have been an enjoyable way, if not to waste time, certainly as a way to fill up some period when, otherwise, I would have been staring out of my office window. Thomas Merton (again!) ends his *Seven Storey Mountain* with the little Latin tag: *finis libri sed non quaerendi.* My sentiments completely: this little book is finished, but not the search.